Christmas Curiosities

Odd, Dark, and Forgotten Christmas

John Grossman

STEWART, TABORI & CHANG
NEW YORK

Dedicated to Carolyn Grossman

Published in 2008 by Stewart, Tabori & Chang
An imprint of Harry N. Abrams, Inc.

Image digital file preparation by Carolyn Grossman

Library of Congress Cataloging-in-Publication Data:

Grossman, John.
Christmas curiosities : odd, dark, and forgotten Christmas / John Grossman.
p. cm.
Includes bibliographical references.
ISBN-13: 978-1-58479-699-2
ISBN-10: 1-58479-699-5
1. Christmas—History. 2. Santa Claus—History. 3. Christmas in art. 4. Postcards. I. Title.
GT4985.G77 2008
394.2663—dc22

2007040771

Editor: Dervla Kelly
Designer: Kay Schuckhart/Blond on Pond
Production Manager: Tina Cameron

The text of this book was composed in Adobe Caslon, Archive Tale, and Neutra Text Book.

Printed and bound in China
10 9 8 7 6 5 4 3 2 1

115 West 18th Street
New York, NY 10011
www.hnabooks.com

Contents

Christmas Greetings

Christmas As You've Never Known It

runken rowdies roaming the streets at night in New York and Philadelphia, banging pots, pans, and drums, blowing horns and whistles, making raucous noises, and creating as much racket as possible. In the South, gunfire and firecrackers, all-day drinking by all classes, more horn-blowing and hell-raising.

Home invasion—masked people, most of them young men, poor or from the working class, entering houses with impunity, doing little skits, demanding gifts of food, drink, or money, threatening broken windows or worse unless they got it.

Public feasting, gluttony, and drunkenness everywhere.

This was the Christmas season in early America around 1800, before Santa Claus, before decorating Christmas trees, Christmas shopping, family gift giving, and all the other familiar activities now associated with Christmas. The holiday season was then more of a public celebration in the streets and alehouses rather than one quietly observed at home around the family hearth.

The winter nights were long and dark. Oil lamps, candles, torches, and the fireplace were the only sources of light to keep back the shifting shadows. In many parts of Europe, those shadows were believed to include

A concern of respectable people in the early nineteenth century, whether in Boston or London, was the "idleness and dissipation" of young boys, generally working class, during the holidays. Snowballing was especially popular among gangs of young miscreants hanging around neighborhood street corners making noise, drinking, firing guns, and playing tricks on people. This was especially threatening to upright citizens who could and did get hurt by snowballs.

malicious spirits, demons, and other threatening entities. These had to be appeased by gifts, and precautions had to be taken to drive them off—ringing church bells, sprinkling holy water in the corners of the house, burning logs in the fireplace all night, and making loud noises. Venturing into the night was frightening and to be avoided at all costs, since folk beliefs in parts of northern Europe claimed that bears, werewolves, and trolls were out and about.

The Twelve Days of Christmas, December 25 to January 6 (Epiphany), declared a sacred season of celebration by the Council of Troyes in 567, had become in the minds of the ordinary people a period during which spirits and supernatural forces roamed the earth.

The old pagan gods seemed never far. During the winter solstice, it was believed that the Norse god Thor rode through the skies in a chariot pulled by two goats, distributing gifts to the Vikings. His father, Odin (or Wodin), rode a white eight-legged steed, escorting slain heroes into Valhalla. Some of the gods' aspects are thought to have become incorporated into the folk figures of various giftbringers, including Santa Claus.

Romans celebrated a midwinter festival, Saturnalia, from December 17 to December 23, during which the roles of master and servant were reversed, and societal rules were turned on end, resulting in much rowdy revelry. The early church heartily disapproved of the whole thing and around 350 A.D. chose to co-opt the pagans by declaring December 25 Christ's day of birth, successfully making it a Christian festival.

Over the centuries travel and communication had been very slow, allowing local traditions to be formed and sustained—every person, every society, every country had different views of what Christmas was, how it was celebrated, and how it looked.

Printed material was limited and expensive right up to the beginning of the nineteenth century. Few ordinary people could afford books. Prints, mostly engraved and sometimes hand colored, could be afforded only by the landed gentry, wealthy individuals, and, in Europe, the nobility. Crude woodcut popular prints were peddled in the cities, but even those were too costly for most of the common people.

By the end of the nineteenth century, in astonishing contrast, a revolution in printing technology had taken place, bringing inexpensive color printed materials to average citizens everywhere.

Merchants were giving away such things as beautifully printed full-color calendars, illustrated with appealing subjects, including Christmas, often embossed and die-cut, proudly imprinted with the merchant's name, free to their customers.

The look of Christmas began to manifest increasingly in printed form, with legions of artists creating their own conceptions of the seasonal celebration, distributed in the form of popular visual culture as advertising materials, greeting cards, sheet music, book and magazine illustrations, and, later, postcards.

But consensus about such things as what the Christmas giftbringer looked like was long in developing—and certainly curious.

A little night music. During the Christmas season in eighteenth-century England and the United States, the incredibly loud and annoying "music" of roving callithumpian bands—the *thump* part of the name being especially descriptive—kept respectable citizens awake with incessant banging of pots and pans, rude noises, shouting, catcalls, beating drums, blowing horns, and discordant playing of any handy instrument. Another form of nighttime serenading in Britain was performed by groups of instrumentalists—minus the pots and pans and loutish noises—and singers known as "the waits," who went from house to house playing in exchange for food, drink, and tips. Some waits were licensed by the towns.

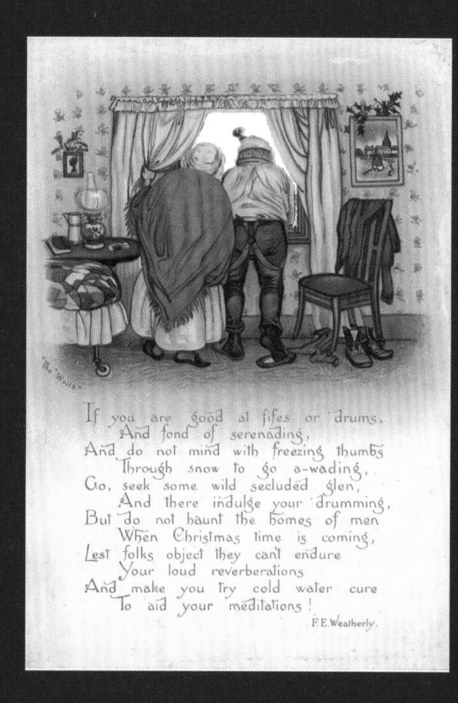

→ No, thank you, and scram. The reverse side of the same card, from around 1890, shows the low regard in which the amateur seasonal serenaders were held. By the end of the nineteenth century, the waits as well as other holiday begging practices finally came to an end

← Not all householders welcomed the nocturnal bands outside their windows, especially if the performers were an impromptu bunch and of meager talent. Here, Mr. and Mrs. Scrooge, who were just getting ready for bed, are having a look out their window at the street musicians jamming below.

Christmas roast rat. A great feast being prepared by fur-clad elves and fairies in a frozen fairyland. This was a world many Victorians firmly believed existed; they would have expected the wee folk to celebrate the season just like humans.

Food fight. The holiday feast so immensely enjoyed by Victorians had two new dishes in competition with the traditional roast goose or roast beef—a fat round plum pudding and roast turkey. Eating and stuffing oneself during the Christmas season, washing it all down with quantities of liquors, was a time-honored activity dating back to the Middle Ages and the great feasts of roast beef, boars' heads, larks' tongue pies, capons, and bowls of wassail set out by the lords of the manors.

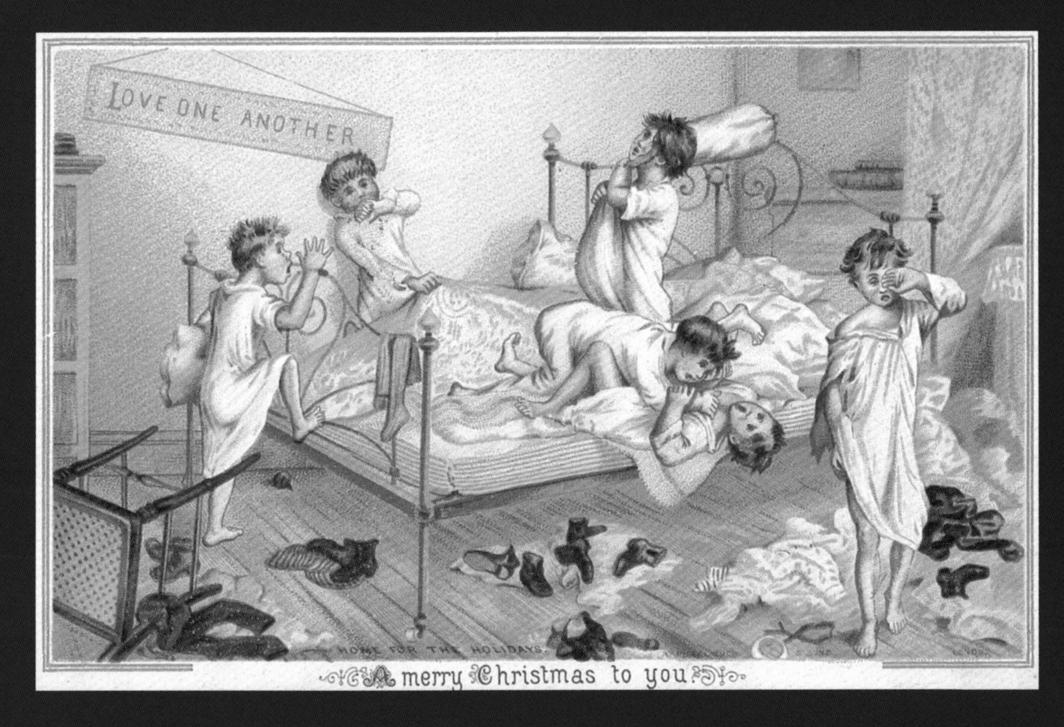

"Love one another." More boys acting up during the holidays: a raging pillow fight in a school dormitory, the headmaster absent. But then, what do you expect when there are six boys to a bed? Boys will be boys and all that.

Girls are almost never—make that never—shown misbehaving at this level of disorder in the imagery of the period; they're only naughty or disobedient.

A Merry
Christmas
and
a
Happy
New Year.

The dark side of Christmas. People got it into their heads, particularly in old Europe, that during the Twelve Days of Christmas witches and various threatening spirits flitted around in the winter skies. It was thought that the dark forces roamed the earth at this time intending to do evil because they were enraged at the celebration of the Savior's birth. Means were devised to keep the evil spirits at bay. Fires were kept burning all night to prevent witches from coming down the chimney. In Norway, brooms were put away so witches could not ride off on them. The sign of the cross was painted in tar over doorways to protect the house and barn. Not all witches were bad, though: in Italy, the old crone Befana rode about on her broom bringing gifts to children on Epiphany Eve.

Cherub bat jockeys. By the end of the nineteenth century, the evil spirits, witches, and goblins lurked no more at night during the Twelve Days of Christmas. The old superstitions were fading fast under the scrutiny of a rational age. But Victorian whimsy knew no bounds, and the seasonal sentimentality remained: owls, bats, and other night creatures still appeared—in amusing and nonthreatening ways, as on this card from the late 1890s.

The Sainted Giftbringer

ost children waking up in America today on the morning of December 6 to find their stockings filled with treats and toys would think that old Santa had finally gotten Alzheimer's.

But in Holland and Belgium and other European countries, all would be well, for St. Nicholas had arrived the night before December 6, St. Nicholas Day, and rewarded all the good children right on schedule.

Unlike some of the mythic folk giftbringers that gave rise to the Santa Claus figure, St. Nicholas was a real person, known to have lived during the fourth century, born in Patara, in what is now Turkey. He began a religious career, advancing from serving as a monk in a monastery in Myra, a town now called Demre, to bishop at an early age, finally rising to the rank of archbishop of Myra.

Beyond a few other facts, nearly everything written about his life is based on legends. Signs of his holiness were said to begin at his birth, when he immediately stood up to praise God and later refused his mother's milk on fast days.

He was to become the world's most popular non-Biblical saint, with more than two thousand churches dedicated to him in France and

Perhaps a little rushed, the good saint leans over the window sill and dumps the treats on the floor, completely missing the shoes and boots, a sometime giftbringer practice known as "pick-'em-ups."

Germany and four hundred in England. Artists have portrayed him more than any other saint except Mary. He is the patron saint of, among many others, banking, pawnbroking, scholarship, pirating, butchery, sailing, thievery, haberdashery, and of orphans and royalty—and New York City.

Nicholas is described as having been quite wealthy from inheritance. He became known, despite his efforts to be anonymous, for secretly giving away his wealth to the needy.

One legend repeatedly retold about one of his acts of charity is claimed to be the source for the custom of hanging up stockings and giving gifts at Christmastime. A desperate father had lost his wealth and could no longer provide dowries for his three daughters, which at the time meant that they were unmarriageable and likely to be forced into the streets and prostitution. Nicholas heard of the dilemma, and on each of three nights in a row, he secretly tossed a bag of gold through the window of the man's house, to ensure that his daughters would have their dowries. Instead of landing on the hearth, the bags fell into stockings hung up to dry.

Besides his generosity and kindness, Nicholas was also credited with miraculous powers, as often retold in a very dark tale. During a visit to an inn, Nicholas detected that the criminal innkeeper had stolen all the money carried by three traveling students while they slept, killed them, then cut them up into pieces and hidden the parts in pickle barrels to conceal his crime. Outraged, Nicholas reassembled their bodies and restored the students to life. For this and other similar miracles, he became the patron saint of students and children.

St. Nicholas is said to have died on December 6, which was to become St. Nicholas Day as proclaimed by the church, a day of celebration and gift giving among Roman Catholics.

In addition to the real persecution, imprisonment, and torture Nicholas suffered later in his life at the hands of the Romans in the fourth century, in the sixteenth century he suffered serious loss of veneration during the Protestant Reformation and its war on the cult of the saints. Protestants replaced him as the giftbringer, first with the Christ Child and then with a host of secularized figures. The gift-giving time was moved from December 6 to December 25 or New Year's Day.

SANCTE CLAUS goed heylig Man!
Trek uwe beste Tabaert aen,
Reiz daer me'e na Amsterdam,
Van Amsterdam na 'Spanje,
Daer Appelen van Oranje,
Daer Appelen van granaten,
Die rollen door de Straaten.
SANCTE CLAUS, myn goede Vriend!
Ik heb U allen tyd gedient,
Wille U my nu wat geven,
Ik zal U dienen alle myn Leven.

Saint Nicholas, good holy man!
Put on the Tabard,* best you can,
Go, clad therewith, to Amsterdam,
From Amsterdam to Hispanje,
Where apples *bright* † of Oranje,
And likewise those *granate* ‡ surnam'd,
Roll through the streets, all free unclaim'd.
Saint Nicholas, my dear good friend!
To serve you ever was my end,
If you will, now, me something give,
I'll serve you ever while I live.

* Kind of jacket. † Oranges. ‡ Pomegranates.

The earliest printed image known of the historic St. Nicholas in America is this 1810 broadside. An early New York City cultural activist, John Pintard (1759–1844), commissioned it to be engraved on wood as a memento of the first annual celebration of the Festival of St. Nicholas on December 6, 1810. A stern and commanding figure in his ecclesiastical robes, St. Nicholas holds a birch rod, not his traditional crosier, or bishop's staff. Pintard was one of the respectable citizens thoroughly alarmed at the young drunken rowdies celebrating Christmas in the streets and was likely more interested in St. Nicholas as a symbol of discipline and punishment than as an emblem of his churchly office. On the right is shown the good little girl with her gifts, next to her the badly behaved boy with his present of the birch rod. *Collection of the New-York Historical Society.*

➛ Shoes and boots, not stockings, were put out at windows or doorways by Austrian children for St. Nicholas to fill. Here a boy has put his boots out just in time, as the saint is about to round the corner. Pictured on a 1905 postcard printed in Germany and mailed to a child in Washington from his aunt and uncle in California, this European custom apparently did not seem strange at the time in the land of Santa Claus.

➛ Gifts for adults were nicely wrapped and hand delivered by St. Nicholas, at least in this conception from around 1910. Around 1880, as gift exchanges became more popular, people began to wrap their increasingly store-bought purchases in white tissue or decorative paper tied with colorful ribbon or tinsel cord, to make—surprise—the commercially made gift look more special.

➤ St. Nicholas presents a hopeful swain with the woman of his dreams in miniature, served up on a heart-shaped gingerbread cookie.

➤ A more businesslike St. Nicholas in the same 1906 postcard series whips out a miniature suitor doll for a pleased young woman from among the gifts carried in a gathering of his robe. She would consider the doll a sign that she'd be married in the coming year.

Groeten
van St. Nicolaas

The ship carrying St. Nicholas, Sinterklaas, from Spain has docked at Amsterdam in Holland and now the saint is being transported through the streets to great acclaim in a carriage pulled by white horses. More typically, he rides a white horse himself. His helper, Black Peter, a Moor traditionally dressed as a sort of sixteenth-century Spanish page and who used to be a much more menacing character, walks alongside. They have arrived weeks before the saint's official feast day, December 6, and will have a busy round of appearances. Dutch folklore maintains that Nicholas and Black Peter fly across Holland, mounted on the saint's magical white horse, to deliver gifts to children on St. Nicholas's Eve. Just to make things more interesting, according to Dutch tradition St. Nicholas was born in Spain, not Asia Minor.

From the beginning of the nineteenth century and the 1810 black-and-white broadside of an ascetic St. Nicholas (page 26), we come to the end of the century and this richly colorful St. Nicholas as Santa Claus—or is this Santa Claus as St. Nicholas?

A very realistic St. Nicholas is receiving the prayers of children before handing out the sweets. This was the very thing Protestants had long objected to—the worship of saints and St. Nicholas—and it brought about a historic schism in Catholic versus Protestant conceptions of the giftbringers. More to come about the figure in red behind the saint.

By 1920, the approximate date of this children's scrap picture, a new concept in giftbringers had appeared: *both* St. Nicholas and Santa Claus arrive to give gifts to children, neatly resolving objections to having either a religious figure or a secular one as the giftbringer.

When the Devil Came to Christmas

truly astonishing accomplishment of St. Nicholas was his later enlistment of the Devil as his helper when making his rounds on the eve of December 6. At least the dark figure lurking behind the good bishop certainly looked like the Devil—horns, hooves, black fur, tail, chains, long red tongue, malicious expression, brandishing switches or a whip.

In Europe, especially the Germanic countries, this devil figure was known by many folk names—Knecht Ruprecht, Krampus, Hans Trapp, Black Peter, Klaubauf, Hans Muff, Butz—and was employed as a helper to deal directly with badly behaved children at Christmas. St. Nicholas gave out the treats of nuts, fruits, and cookies to the good children. Krampus, right behind him, delivered birch rods and ashes to the wrongdoers.

The historic St. Nicholas would never believe his eyes at this later association of Satan with his person. How had *this* come about?

Scholars speculate that the origins of the bogeymen can be traced back to ancient times, to pagan deities and fertility spirits who were associated with the winter solstice celebrations and who were said to prowl the countryside during the long, cold, dark nights.

Others suggest that the near obsession with the Devil and all his works by Protestants, who felt him to be a malevolent physical being to be

Gruß vom
Krampus

constantly reckoned with, assigned him to St. Nicholas in a position of submission and subservience, confirming God's power over evil.

Or maybe it all boils down to parents of olden times simply wanting to find a surrogate figure to scare the bejesus out of their ungovernable children, generally boys, and make them behave.

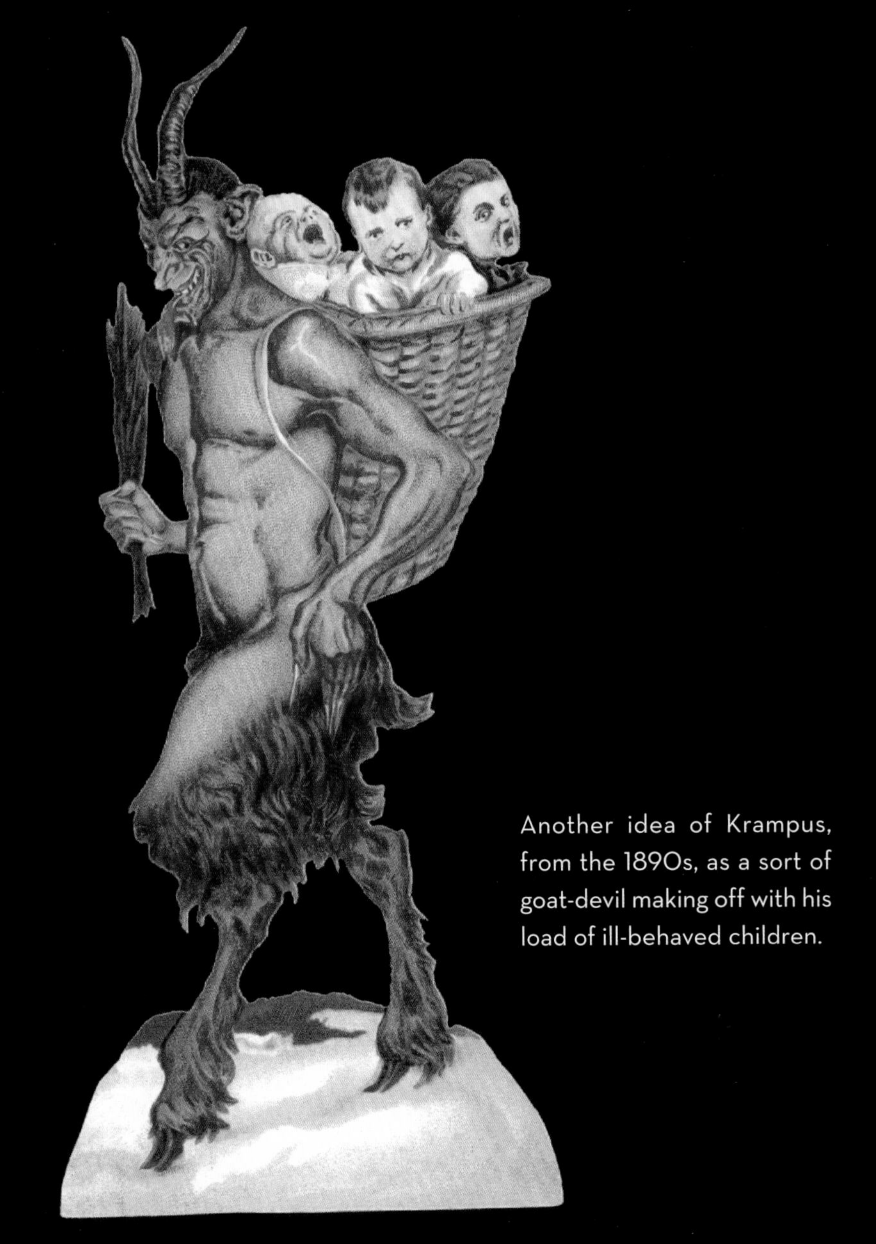

Another idea of Krampus, from the 1890s, as a sort of goat-devil making off with his load of ill-behaved children.

This 1899 postcard from Vienna says it all: the holy bishop St. Nicholas dispensing pastries and fruits to the good little girls in prayerful attitudes, his helper angel beside him, perhaps representing the Christ Child—and two little boys hiding under the table from the menacing Krampus right outside the door. The Dachshund is on high alert.

This tableau comes from an 1881 American children's book, *Around the World with Santa-Claus*, which richly illustrated the Christmas traditions of other nations. Here are all the main Christmas characters in Germany: the Christ Child, St. Nicholas, St. Peter—and the bogeyman, Black Rupert, also known as Krampus. American kids must have been fascinated. There was no tradition in America of a devil figure accompanying St. Nicholas—just a benevolent Santa Claus.

Krampus bursting through from Hell to grab the naughty boy praying for deliverance was part of a series of four postcards printed in Germany around 1910 that were clearly intended to be distributed in the United States but were probably limited to German-American communities—Krampus was hardly an American folk figure.

"Greetings from Krampus." Not a good sign: Krampus is pulling the strings in this courtship. He was known to cart off adults as well as children. Around 1905, Krampus began to be shown as having a life of his own, independent of St. Nicholas.

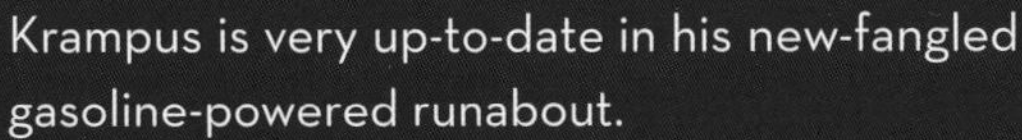
Krampus is very up-to-date in his new-fangled gasoline-powered runabout.

The final destination—the fiery pit. Krampus may have been the servant of the Catholic St. Nicholas, but he fit right in with the Protestant concern with the Day of Judgment and hellfire and damnation. Children must have wet their pants when seeing this 1911 card.

Czech children feared the dreaded Cert, another name for the devil figure, Krampus. All the Krampus attributes are here: black fur, long red tongue, horns, tail, one leg with a furry foot, and the

Yes! A female Krampus. With a refined gold chain, a tease of a red tongue, and a basketful of dandies, she holds switches in a black-gloved hand. This muted suggestion of a dominatrix probably gave some men a little frisson, but the card was actually addressed to a woman. The image may have appealed to women as representing a little female power over men in an otherwise paternalistic age.

Another female "Krampus," vital, athletic, striding purposefully along, her basket filled with several Krampus dolls and one of St. Nicholas. Is she taking away the old male giftbringer and his male demonic servant to be rid of them? This liberated young woman only represents a Krampus; she is in costume, the horns being part of her hat.

Santa, We Hardly Know Ye

Santa Claus? Of course we know who he is—everyone does, nearly the world over, from American movies and TV and other media. He is a jolly, fat, grandfatherly man with a long white beard, a red suit and cap trimmed in white fur, a wide belt, boots, gloves, and a big sack of toys slung over his shoulder. He arrives from the North Pole in a sleigh pulled by reindeer, dropping down chimneys to bring gifts to children on Christmas Eve.

This wasn't always so. Our ancestors in the nineteenth century hadn't really made up their minds about the look of the man. He was just being invented in America. They enjoyed many representations of him by artists of the period, and each had their own ideas about how Santa looked and how he performed his Christmas Eve rounds.

The first written description of St. Nicholas in America was by Washington Irving (1783–1859), in his famous 1809 mock chronicle, *Knickerbocker's History of New York*: "in the sylvan days of New Amsterdam [New York], the good St. Nicholas would often make his appearance in his beloved city, of a holiday afternoon, riding [in a wagon drawn by a horse] jollily among the treetops, or over the roofs of houses, now and then drawing forth magnificent presents from his breeches pockets, and dropping them down the chimneys of his favorites."

1821. The first illustration of Santa Claus in America, a small lithographed and hand-colored book, "The Children's Friend"—printed in New York, authored and illustrated anonymously—seemingly out of the blue showed "Old Santeclaus" as a smallish fur-clad figure in a sleigh pulled by a reindeer, on a snowy rooftop, delivering "rewards." There had been no drawn or written description of a gift-bringer with all of these attributes. Washington Irving had described St. Nicholas in 1809 as basically looking like a Dutch burgher, flying over the rooftops in a wagon drawn by a horse. The St. Nicholas broadside of 1810 (page 26) showed a stern bishop. There is no known record of how this new figure came to be as pictured in this little book, but it is clearly the beginning of the American Santa Claus—and it appeared before Clement C. Moore wrote "A Visit from St. Nicholas" in 1822. *Courtesy of the American Antiquarian Society.*

This was definitely not the Santa Claus we now know, not even the traditional St. Nicholas. The Dutch had brought their familiar St. Nicholas with them to the New World in the seventeenth century, for some reason leaving Black Peter behind. Irving's description of St. Nicholas stripped him of his bishop robes, tall miter, crosier, and sober, saintly demeanor, and transformed him into the image of a Dutch burgher, short, round, jolly, smoking a long-stemmed clay pipe and dressed in colonial garb.

The formal Dutch name for St. Nicholas, Sint Nikolaas, was later slurred by American children into Sinterklaas and then Santa Claus.

A very rare small book, "The Children's Friend," published in 1821 by an anonymous author, is the first American book about Christmas. A fur-clad "Santeclaus" is pictured on the rooftops in a sleigh drawn by a single reindeer.

This is quite a jump from Irving's St. Nicholas—in twelve years without any other appearance, the American giftbringer is now "Santeclaus" and has a sleigh, a reindeer, and a fur suit. There is no known record of exactly how this has come about—folklore is formed and communicated by people in unrecorded ways until eventually an artist or author gathers the threads together and puts them down on paper.

So it is with another famous literary work, the 1822 poem "A Visit from St. Nicholas," claimed to have been written (there is scholarly debate about this) by the American scholar and poet Clement Clark Moore (1779–1863). St. Nicholas is now described as "chubby and plump, a right jolly old elf," and "dressed all in furs from his head to his foot." He also has a white beard, smokes a pipe, has a bundle of toys on his back, and a tiny sleigh pulled by eight miniature reindeer, each of whom now has a name.

Presumably St. Nicholas is small so he can drop down a chimney. His association with the world of elves and fairies gives him magical powers. The fur suit has likely been taken from the Pennsylvania Dutch

Pelznickol, or "Fur Nicholas," a somewhat menacing fur-clad Christmas folk figure imported to America by the German community to help keep their children in line. Clearly, Moore compiled his St. Nicholas from many sources to give the giftbringer his immortal form.

History now recognizes that the American invention of Santa Claus was under way early in the nineteenth century. Yet depictions of Santa Claus during the first half of the century varied wildly, despite the literary descriptions provided by Irving and Moore, as each artist tried his hand at fashioning a likeness of the new folk figure. Some were pretty odd. Most were still printed in black and white, but there were considerably more of them because printing was becoming cheaper and easier following the invention in 1796 of the lithographic process and its rapid development in the first half of the nineteenth century.

Thomas Nast (1840–1902), a German immigrant from Bavaria, brought his considerable abilities as an illustrator and his family's love of a German Christmas to New York in 1846. He was employed by *Harper's Illustrated Weekly* as a staff artist in 1862, becoming one of its most popular artists, his drawings rendered by others into the complex medium of wood engravings. He produced his first conception of Santa Claus for *Harper's* in 1862 during his first year at the magazine. It was the beginning of a long annual series, lasting until 1886, much beloved by the public. Nast's work became the next important step in the invention of Santa Claus, creating an image of him that is very much recognizable to us today: fat, jolly, elderly, a kindly bearded face, a belt around his ample middle, and dressed in a fur suit and fur cap, as in Moore's description.

By the second half of the century, full-color lithography came into being and with it came a flood of inexpensive color printed imagery. Now artists could portray Santa in living color. Brown fur suits became a little boring, and by 1900 people had a rich palette of Santa figures to choose from, mostly imported from Germany in the form of the new postal innovation of the postcard, in tunics of every color—yellow, green, blue, black, white, orange, purple—and red. Red was already the preferred color of Santa's costume in children's books by the 1890s, and the look of the American Santa was finally set around the turn of the twentieth century. He has since become the universal Christmas icon.

1841. Twenty years after "Santeclaus" appeared in "The Children's Friend," this woo
engraving of St. Nicholas was published in the New York weekly papers *Brother Jonatha*
and the *New-York Mirror*. Reverting back to Washington Irving's 1809 description of th
giftbringer, the artist has pictured him as a sort of middle-aged Dutchman in eighteenth
century clothing, with a short beard, almost a goatee, a short pipe, and a basket of toys o
his back. He is about to go down the chimney, and a sleigh awaits him, but with only tw
reindeer. There is very little other evidence of Moore's description of St. Nicholas.

1844. Back to calling him Santa Claus. Here he wears a coat trimmed in fur, smokes a pipe, has a short beard, and wears a fur cap. The cross on his cap suggests that there is still a bit of the saint about him in this engraving for the *New-York Mirror*.

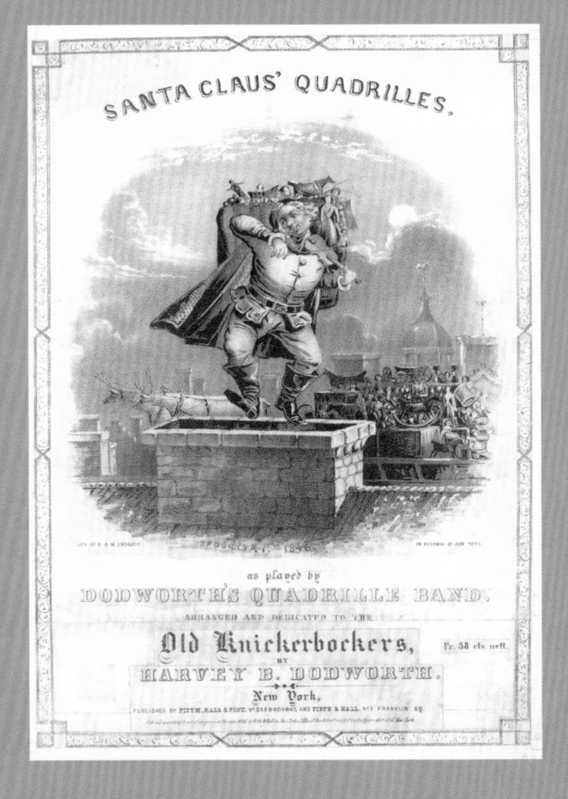

1846. Published in New York, this lithographed sheet music cover illustration of Santa Claus (the name again) shows the costume influence of Washington Irving's Dutch St. Nicholas conception. The music was, after all, dedicated to the "Old Knickerbockers," an antiquarian-minded patrician class of men who'd had much to do with the invention of Santa Claus in early America. Washington Irving was a member. But this is a very unique vision of Santa Claus, never to be seen again: a young, beardless man, dancing and playing a fiddle.

1846/1884. An 1846 painting, *Santa Claus, or St. Nicholas*, by Robert Weir (1803–1889), that was reproduced in 1884 as a chromolithograph, shown here. Weir was an accomplished painter, drawing instructor, and, later, a National Academician; his 1837 version of the scene was the first American painting of Santa. Interestingly, it included long switches slung on Santa's pack, which Weir eliminated in this 1846 version. The three stockings hung by the fireplace are for Weir's own family: the large stocking on the far right, filled with yarn and needles, is for his wife; the next, stuffed with toys and good things to eat, is for one of his sons; the stocking on the left has only a switch and is for his other son, little Walter Weir—but dangling from the toe is a jumping jack, as a sort of consolation. Weir's Santa still shows the Dutch influence: short and stout, big boots, a clay pipe in his cap. But he is about to ascend the chimney, finger alongside his nose, as in Moore's famous 1822 poem. He is a transitional figure.

1848. Now comes the rare first book-length edition of Moore's poem, "A Visit from St. Nicholas," illustrated by New York wood engraver Theodore Boyd (1830-?). Never mind Moore's description of St. Nick as a "right jolly old elf," "dressed all in furs from his head to his foot"—Boyd ignores all that and reverts to Washington Irving's 1809 plebeian Dutch St. Nicholas, eighteenth-century garb and all. What's a person to think? *Courtesy of the Clarke Historical Library, Central Michigan University.*

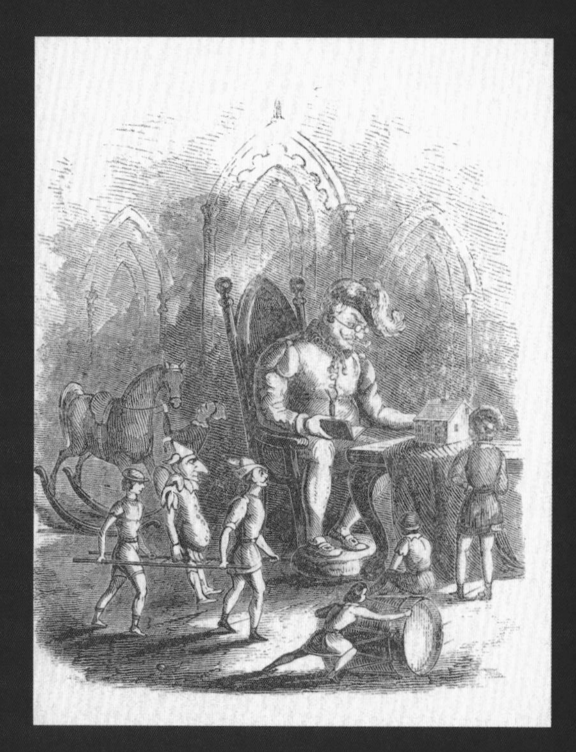

1850. Things are still a little confused as to just what Santa Claus looks like, as in this wood-engraved illustration from the children's book *Messenger Birds*, by Caroline H. Butler, published in Boston. Aside from the remarkable appearance of Santa in Renaissance dress, sitting in a gothic-style chair, he is now shown with elves as helpers—the author calls them "little work-people"—in his toy-manufacturing business.

1868. A Thomas Nast illustration from the children's book *Santa Claus and His Works*, published by McLoughlin Bros., New York. Once inexpensive full-color printing became possible, the children's book industry took off. Nast, reveling in color after all his years of producing black-and-white illustrations for Harper's Weekly, has Santa making his own toys. Later, he would make the fur suit more red.

Circa 1870. A children's book cover by Thomas Nast for Clement Moore's poem (but no credit given to Moore). The long clay pipe is the last vestige of Washington Irving's Dutch St. Nicholas.

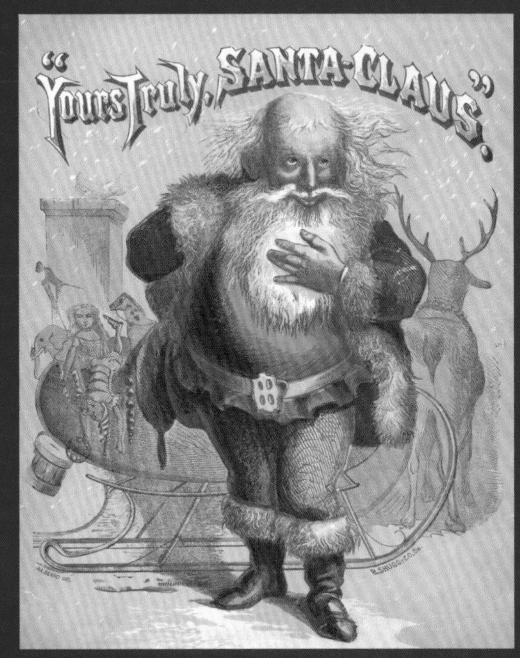

1872. Santa without his cap is revealed to be nearly bald by James C. Beard (1837–1913) for the children's book *A Merry Christmas*, with an original story by "Aunt Lutie."

← **1879.** Another children's book illustration for Moore's poem, retitled *Santa Claus; or, the Night before Christmas*, by an unidentified artist. This Santa could be considered an elf, but despite the description in the poem, his outfit is trimmed in fur rather than all fur, and he has a cute little white goatee.

Circa 1880. Still another publisher—unidentified—tried its hand at producing a children's book of Moore's poem. The artist, J. B. Geyser, has added a new touch: a youngish-looking Mrs. Claus in a long, ornate robe seeing Santa off from their abode at the North Pole.

1882. Santa, looking just a bit shaggy, all "dressed in furs from his head to his foot" in the tradition of Moore's poem, is on the cover of a shaped gift book of poems, edited by Julia Caroline née Ripley Dorr, an American writer best known for her own poems. The brown fur suit persisted alongside the red suit popularized by Nast. Red was increasingly preferred in children's books and of course ultimately won out because that's what the kids liked and publishers noticed that the red attracted attention.

Circa 1880. An altogether different group of illustrators from those employed for children's books—advertising artists—came up with some very unusual ideas about Santa's appearance. This stock image of a grotesque dwarflike Santa with large teeth clamped on a hardwood pipe was intended to be imprinted with a merchant's name, but never was. Whether it was sufficiently appealing to people to move goods is questionable, but the toys tucked into the tops of the boots is a nice touch.

Circa 1885. Advertising art in the form of a large shaped folder, shown unfolded, with Santa completely outfitted in black fur. If it weren't for that little detail he would look pretty much like Santa does today. "Wm. H. Frear, The Trojan Santa Claus," imprinted on the rug, refers to Frear's store, located in Troy, New York (the inhabitants of ancient Troy were called Trojans).

Circa 1890. This late-period brown-fur-suited Santa seems more like an ogre with a bad eye indicating he is about to go down there and frighten the kids silly. And maybe the parents too—if they'd even let him in the house. Good thing he is wearing the sleigh bells, and not the deer, so everyone will be warned that he is coming. This was a large (thirteen-inch-high) shaped advertising giveaway from George Heather's Fancy Goods Store in New York City, and one wonders why it was thought the image would be broadly appealing, other than the spectacular load of toys.

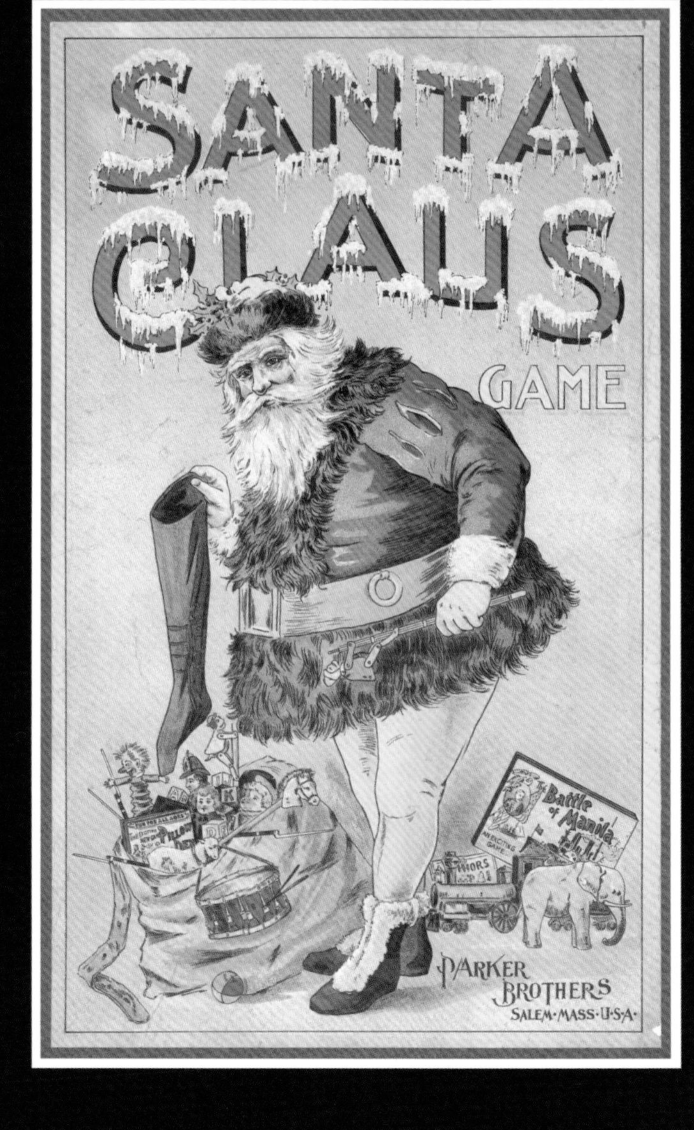

Circa 1900. Some artists still by this time had not succumbed to the inevitable red-suited, white-fur-trimmed Santa. On this game box lid, Santa is instead wearing a stylish ensemble featuring rich brown fur trim on his red coat, a blue sash for a belt, fabulous yellow tights, and trim little galoshes edged in elegant white fur.

A Pantheon of Giftbringers

Once St. Nicholas had been deposed as the Christmas gift-bringer by the Protestants during the Reformation in seventeenth-century Germany, the reformers soon realized a substitution for the saint would be needed—and pretty quickly. Their children would not be denied the excitement and joy of receiving gifts left during the night by an unseen, mysterious, loving and generous visitor. A remarkable progression of stand-ins for St. Nicholas came into being over the next centuries, some still appearing today.

The first **Christ Child**, or **Christkindl** (Le Petit Noël in France, El Niño in Spanish America), was originally promoted by Martin Luther and his Protestant followers to teach children that all blessings come from God through Christ. Originally imagined as the Child Jesus himself, the Christkindl mutated over time into an angel who appears as a young girl in a flowing white robe, with wings and a radiant halo.

The Christkindl came to the United States with German immigrants, but as the lore and custom faded in the new land, *Christkindl* became *Kriss Kringle*, and finally just another name for Santa Claus.

Concerns in the religious community that Santa Claus and his European derivatives were becoming just a little too secular resulted in the Christ Child sometimes being portrayed as accompanying Santa on

The Christ Child, or *Christkindl*, as the giftbringer, but also as the Good Shepherd, and with his symbol, the Lamb of God, bearing the gifts.

his rounds, an almost political solution to the Christmas folk figure controversy.

Angels, literally messengers from God, have always been an important part of Christmas, beginning with their role in the Nativity story. They were pressed into service as giftbringers by the culture of the nineteenth century, much as the Christ Child had been back in the seventeenth century.

They were sometimes portrayed as helpers to Santa in various ways, and can also be interpreted as another form of the Christ Child when depicted as a child angel.

Father Christmas, sometimes called King Christmas, Sir Christmas, or Old Christmas, is the personification of Christmas in the British Isles, and has a long, rather convoluted pedigree dating back to the Middle Ages, when Christmas was celebrated with great feasting, drink, and merriment. Sometimes described as hale and hearty, even fat, other times thin, gray, and bearded, he represented the abundance and good cheer of the season. In the seventeenth century, the revelry and excesses during the season irritated the sober English Puritans greatly, who condemned it all as nothing but the old Roman celebration of Saturnalia, and believed that there was no Biblical basis for Christmas feast days. Or even, for that matter, for Christmas itself, since the actual date of Christ's birth is unknown.

Puritans finally succeeded in outlawing the whole Christmas business when they gained control of Parliament in 1644, executing the king in 1649 for treason—and, effectively, Father Christmas, for undue merriment. Severe punishments were inflicted upon anyone who celebrated Christmas in any way whatsoever. Riots and brawls sometimes broke out against the enforcers. Christmas went underground.

King Charles II finally restored Christmas and other religious observances in 1660 when he ascended the throne following the collapse of the Puritan Protectorate. Father Christmas was back, but he was a little subdued.

By the nineteenth century, in some representations he appears rather like a roaring public drunk, wineglass held high, wearing a long fur-trimmed robe, sometimes with a hood, a crown of holly on his head, and a flushed, excited expression. He began to be associated more with giftbringing and less with merrymaking under the increasing influence and competition of America's Santa Claus, who ultimately absorbed him—Father Christmas kept his name but became Santa Claus.

Père Noël is France's Father Christmas and personification of Christmas. He was unknown in France before the first half of the nineteenth century, although there had been Christmas personifications in France dating back to the thirteenth century. While Père Noël was a composite of earlier giftbringers, the development and increasing popularity of America's Santa Claus appears to have been a major influence in his creation. His appearance, though, was often quite different from the American prototype—old men as monks, or in robes of blue, red, white, or green, in caps, hoods, and cowls, carrying *hottes* (grape picker's baskets carried on the back), sacks, baskets, rods, and switches. Here and there a little religious imagery persisted, with his robe looking somewhat like that of a bishop, and little angels sometimes fluttering about.

The 1870s were a period of revolt in France against the Catholic Church by Protestants and schoolteachers of the Third Republic who gained effective power over children and an important victory over the clergy. Instead of St. Nicholas, the handy legend of the secular Père Noël as the giftbringer was diffused rapidly by patriotic groups, charitable organizations, and the schools. Eventually he also came to look and act a lot like Santa Claus, much to the great outrage of the Catholic clergy, some of whom condemned him as a heretic and usurper, and burned him in effigy on December 23, 1951, in the square of the cathedral in Dijon.

Weihnachtsmann, or "**Christmasman**," was a nineteenth-century German secularized replacement for St. Nicholas by Protestants, as it was increasingly felt that the Christ Child, the original Protestant substitute, as the Son of God, should not be cast in the role of the giftbringer.

Weihnachtsmann is generally portrayed as a thin, white-bearded old man in a long robe who trudges alone through the snowy Christmas Eve night to deliver gifts to children. He had much in common with the look of Father Christmas and Père Noël, later increasingly having some of Santa's attributes. The variations in his appearance toward the end the nineteenth century and the beginning of the twentieth are astonishing. Germany became a major center of lithography at that time, exporting immense amounts of popular printed Christmas imagery to the United States and all parts of Europe.

Around 1900, when the convenience of the illustrated postcard overcame the sender's squeamishness that others could read his or her written message on the back while the card was in the post, the floodgates were opened to the postcard phenomenon. German artists' conceptions of the Christmasman appeared everywhere—the back of the cards printed in Germany listed the word *postcard* in as many as fourteen languages. Same card, same image, but the greeting changed for the country importing it.

In America, as Santa Claus was rapidly developing into the form we know today, people were happily sending the imported German cards with the wildly varying images of the Christmas giftbringer by the millions to each other, apparently pleased with the variety and flavor they added to the season.

The dominance of the German lithographic industry and its imagery was such that speculation could be made that the Weihnachtsmann, not Santa, would have become the world standard—except that the whole thing was put to an end with World War I. Santa kept marching on.

In Sweden, the **Jultomten** ("Christmas Elf"), a portly gnome with a white beard and a pointed red cap, toting a sack of gifts, was to become the Christmas giftbringer. Similar Christmas elves are known as **Julnissen** in Denmark and **Julenissen** in Norway.

Among other traditional gift-bringers in Europe was the old woman, **La Befana**, in Italy, who came down the chimney on the night of January 5, while in Spanish-speaking countries, the **Magi**, or **Three Kings**, also appeared on the night of January 5.

Women, children, fairies, gnomes, and others were also enlisted to deliver gifts. Children must have started to wonder just who was going to show up with their gifts on Christmas Eve.

An 1884 greeting card evokes a scene of wonder and mystery, as the ethereal Christ Child appears in the night carrying a decorated small tree.

Bright and blest thy Christmas be.

An older, radiant Christ Child in a rich blue robe brings blessings and a tree on a 1909 postcard printed in Germany and mailed in Illinois.

➤ Now properly equipped with a sleigh pulled by a white reindeer, the Christ Child is delivering gifts already wrapped on a postcard printed in Germany and mailed in Petaluma, California, in 1913. During the early years of the twentieth century, the huge German postcard industry was distributing images of the Christmas season worldwide, spreading the various German traditions of giftbringers, including the Christ Child.

➤ Weihnachtsmann, the thin German "Christmasman" smoking his meerschaum pipe, walks alongside the reindeer pulling a sleigh with the Christ Child, the solemn procession led by a gnome lighting the way. This German postcard portrayal of the giftbringer is a long way from Santa's jolly Christmas Eve travels in America, yet it was postmarked in Baltimore, Maryland, in 1911.

← Cigars were popular as a man's gift; it is estimated that four out of five men smoked them at the time of this cigar box label printed in Germany around 1900. The Christ Child has his own little assistant riding along holding a gift box of cigars. The raven, ordinarily a bird of ill omen, adds a curious dark note to this otherwise luminous conception.

→ A much lighter scene shows a very Santa-like Christmasman wearing quilted boots who now personally hauls a sled with the Christ Child. The secular and religious figures shown together tended to quell the objection that the sacred origin of Christmas was being increasingly ignored.

This representation would have been religiously satisfying—a monklike Weihnachtsmann tenderly rocking the cradle of the Christ Child.

Angels from on high. As messengers from God associated with the Nativity, angels were first depicted as male in the Middle Ages, then progressively became more feminine or androgynous until the nineteenth century, when they were finally and invariably shown as female. The Christ Child had sometimes been represented as a young girl in white with wings. From there it was only a short step to angels cast in the role of giftbringers or annunciators of the Christmas season, as on this large 1883 greeting card of an adult female angel in billowing white robes.

A new variant on the angel giftbringer appearance became popular in the 1880s—child angels dressed in all-white winter outfits, known as "snow angels."

The spectacular arrival of a child angel giftbringer in the 1890s.

The little angel helps the big angel make her rounds in 1907.

An angel booth attendant helps two customers make a selection at one of the Christkindl markets held in Germany.

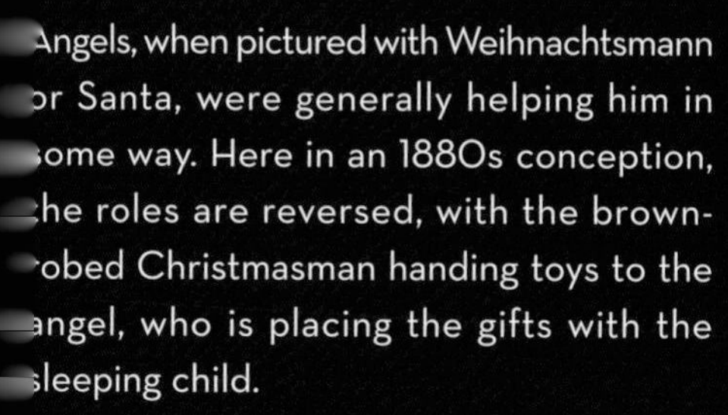

Angels, when pictured with Weihnachtsmann or Santa, were generally helping him in some way. Here in an 1880s conception, the roles are reversed, with the brown-robed Christmasman handing toys to the angel, who is placing the gifts with the sleeping child.

The angel loads up the gift basket as the bundled-up Christmasman reads off his list in this German postcard postmarked 1908 in Franklin, Massachusetts.

The artist of this German cigar box label from around 1900 clearly lifted most of the composition and details from the image on page 81, by another artist, of the child angel as triumphant giftbringer, right down to the elegant white horses. Here, though, the angel is back to being merely a welcoming companion of the brown-robed Weihnachtsmann.

The red-robed gift-bringer gets an earful from a tattletale angel as two miscreants hide behind trees. Parents must have loved this idea.

A Merry Christmas to you.

Father Christmas, wearing his traditional wreath of holly, makes his entrance in a wood engraving published in *The Illustrated London News* in 1866. This is a thoroughly domesticated scene—Father Christmas has clearly put his wilder days as the inebriated Father of the Feast behind him, and is now impersonated by a family member or friend in false whiskers as a giftbringer to the children.

← For a while the English couldn't make up their minds about the true nature of their Christmas folk figure. Historically, he had been the life of the party, not a children's giftbringer. This 1870s greeting card has him up to his old ways, drinking and eating and living it up.

→ As the original Father of the Feast in the Middle Ages, old Father Christmas liked his victuals, and plenty of them, represented here in another 1870s greeting card. No gaunt, gray-bearded old man, but a round, red-suited bon vivant.

"With all his festive fun and cheer," Father Christmas is ready to party in the 1870s. The goat he is riding represents unruly behavior.

By the 1880s, Father Christmas seems a nice old fellow enjoying a ride in a sled playfully pulled by a young woman, with his staff of mistletoe at the ready.

Some of the merriment returns in this greeting card from around 1885.

In the late 1880s there was still no consensus in England as to how Father Christmas should appear, as this scrap picture from the period dramatically shows. Where did he come from? Long green fur-trimmed robe, eighteenth-century shoes, switches, walking stick, hood trimmed with holly, and the visage of an old-time schoolmaster, spectacles and all.

Same period, wildly different figure. There is much of the boisterous, old-time Father Christmas about this one, but now he has a long red robe. As the years continued to roll by, Father Christmas came to look more and more like Santa Claus.

On these two cards from 1877, printed in Paris, Père Noël appears much like the English Father Christmas giftbringer of the same period, with overtones of the good bishop St. Nicholas. Père Noël was also a folk figure that went through changes in appearance, later becoming too much like Santa Claus for some French tastes.

An English gnome in fancy dress using the direct method of gift delivery in the 1870s.

The Jultomten, the small, elderly Swedish Christmas Elf, brings gifts to a child in 1908. Originally, the elf was a mischievous creature who lived under the stairs or in other dark places and required small gifts of food or drink to be left out or there would be pranks.

Gnomes were also pressed into service as gift-bringers, sometimes with a little mishap on the way to delivering the gifts. From a postcard printed in Germany, sent from one child to another in Indiana in 1908.

A snow angel enlists a gnome to carry the load of gifts.

The English love of fairies resulted in this 1880s vision of a ballerina fairy giftbringer emptying an amazing number of presents from one red stocking.

From snow angels as gift-bringers to "snow children" dressed in white winter outfits arriving with gifts.

The Chicago manufacturers of E. T. Gillett's Magic Yeast Cakes gave away this imaginative hanging holiday decoration with each package of their yeast cakes, sometime in the 1880s. One child appears as a variant of a young angel giftbringer (but without wings), the other, who also appears to be a young girl, as a kind of unique child Santa Claus.

A young woman as the giftbringer, riding properly sidesaddle on a deer, as portrayed on a 1902 postcard mailed in France.

American artist R. Ford Harper came straight to the point and fully cast a woman as Santa Claus on this 1913 postcard.

Bringing Switches

s St. Nicholas and his various hideous and threatening dark companions such as Krampus began to fade in importance in Europe, the awful realization must have come to parents that they no longer would have someone to frighten their unruly children into parental obedience at Christmastime.

The solution? Give the switches to the Weihnachtsmann. Let the Christmas giftbringer bring punishment as well as gifts. Which he did, and vigorously—or more often threatened to do, brandishing his bundle of birch rods and raising an admonishing finger. Sometimes he simply stuffed the miscreant into his sack, to be carried off to . . . where?

This dual nature of the giftbringer—both loving and judgmental—gave him God-like qualities. Children were sometimes shown on their knees before him, hands clasped in prayerful attitude, hoping to avoid a sort of juvenile Day of Judgment.

The earliest representation in America of St. Nicholas was as the stern-looking bishop in the 1810 woodcut of the saint holding a birch rod in one hand (page 26). To the right of him is shown a pleased little girl holding her gifts, and next to her a crying little boy holding the rod he got.

In the little 1821 book *The Children's Friend*, "Old Santeclaus" is

Guess who got the switches. The 1890s Weihnachtsmann who administered them is even more forbidding in his very dark purple robe.

pictured for the first time in America (see page 49). After describing the gifts he left for good girls and boys, the book ends with a drawing of two stockings, doubtlessly hung up with care, one of which contains a bundle of switches, and concludes:

But where I found the children naughty
In manners rude, in temper haughty,
Thankless to parents, liars, swearers,
Boxers or base tale-bearers

I left a long, black birchen rod,
Such as the dread command of God
Directs a Parent's hand to use
When virtue's path his sons refuse.

Then a remarkable thing happened in 1822, the following year: in America the switches disappeared altogether from Santa's equipment. Clement Moore's famous poem described Santa as "a right jolly old elf," who filled *all* the stockings with gifts, and left exclaiming, "Happy Christmas to all, and to all a good night."

No judgment, no punishment, but rewards to all, never mind the children's conduct during the year. Santa ever after in America was invariably portrayed as the benevolent spirit of Christmas, with not a switch in sight.

With one unique exception. In nineteenth-century Pennsylvania Dutch country, the German immigrants had brought over their Belsnickle, or Nicholas in furs, originally one of the giftbringer's dark helpers, Knecht Ruprecht. This threatening bearded figure, often arriving alone, dressed in a long fur robe and a pointed hood and carrying a fat bundle of switches, was assigned the task of interrogating children on their behavior during the year. He delivered gifts but also did not spare the rod. By the beginning of the Civil War, both Belsnickle and Christkindl as regional folk figures were well on their way out, to be replaced by Santa Claus.

In Europe, the giftbringer went about as before, delivering both gifts and switches—but fewer and fewer of the switches. The strong influence of the benevolent American Santa, softening views about child rearing, the child-centered home of the second half of the nineteenth century—all combined to make giftbringers everywhere similar in kindliness, tolerance, and love toward children.

The card no kid wanted to get. From *The Game of Kriss Kringle's Visits*, a large, spectacular board game produced by McLoughlin Bros., New York, in 1898, consisting of a Kriss Kringle marker, a spinner, twenty-eight "Gift" cards, and four "Birch Rod" cards. The object of the game—surprise—was to get as many Gift cards as possible. This is a late date for switches and punishment to be associated with Santa Claus in America.

➛ The Pennsylvania Dutch Belsnickle, brought over by German immigrants, was a threatening figure in furs especially fond of carrying a large bundle of switches—and using them. This Belsnickle appeared as the frontispiece for a children's gift book, *The Holiday Album for Boys*, printed in Boston in 1875. He is not mentioned in the text and is likely a stock wood engraving the publisher had had on hand for who knows how long. The Belsnickle had lost out to Santa Claus in most of the nation by this time.

↓ Père Noël, looking much like Santa Claus but certainly not acting like him, stuffing a lazy boy ("Paressel") into his bag in the 1890s.

↑ Another version of Père Noël, laying on the birch rods, imprinted "Chocolat Payraud" on the back—an odd combination of sweets and punishment. The French had their own bogeyman, Père Fouettard, or "Father Whipper," a dark companion to St. Nicholas on St. Nicholas Day who punished bad children with switches or a whip. This Père Noël has taken on Père Fouettard's duties.

An odd old-time-schoolteacher Father Christmas from the late 1880s, with his walking stick, eighteenth-century shoes, and long red robe, brandishes his bundle of switches in the classic warning to be good—*or else*.

The German Christmasman arrives in this thirteen-inch-high scrap picture from the 1890s. The girl probably has little to worry about, but she prays to him just in case, even though he's not really a saint anymore. With switches in hand, one crying boy—always a boy—in the bag, and another underarm, this imposing figure inspires dread, not joy.

➛ Times have certainly changed. Today this Weihnachtsmann would be in the slammer for quite a while after this scene. From an 1890s German children's book, *Weihnachts-Wanderungen*, "Christmas Walking Tours."

A Merry Christmas

This giftbringer may look a lot like Santa in his red outfit, but he acts more like Krampus. A postcard printed in Germany and sent to a Somerville, New Jersey, address in 1907, it was part of the huge influx of German postcards in the early 1900s that brought old European Christmas folk ways for a time to America.

Salesman Santa

fter Clement Moore's 1822 poem began its rise to nearly universal popularity, ensuring Santa's fame, commercial interests saw the potential for having Santa hawk their goods. He was, after all, the giftbringer, described in Moore's poem as carrying "a bundle of toys just over his back / and he looked like a peddler just opening his sack." How perfect was that for promoting Christmas consumerism? Why not have Santa bring gifts from their store or emporium? Or simply be in effect a celebrity who endorses the manufacturer's product?

It took a little while for this to happen. In the early years of the first half of the nineteenth century in the United States, 90 percent of the population lived on farms, made their own things, and didn't have much money to buy anything with anyway.

Also, paper was both expensive to make and scarce. To conserve space in newspapers, the primary advertising medium of the time, ads were set in very small type in dense columns, generally without illustrations, certainly none of Santa. Things began to change by the 1840s, when an 1842 ad appeared three columns wide for "Pease's Great Variety Store" in Albany, New York, illustrated with the same Dutch-looking Santa Claus first published in 1841 in the weekly New York papers *Brother Jonathan* and the *New-York Mirror*.

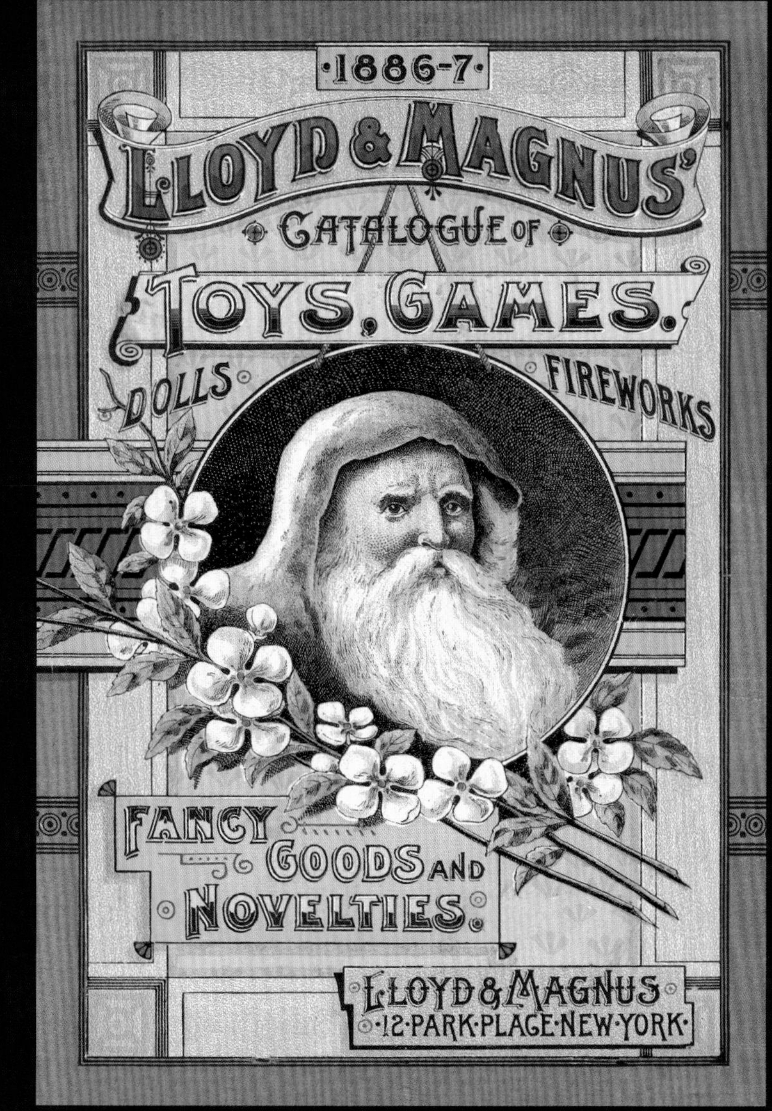
1886-7
LLOYD & MAGNUS'
CATALOGUE OF
TOYS, GAMES.
DOLLS
FIREWORKS
FANCY
GOODS AND
NOVELTIES.
LLOYD & MAGNUS
12 PARK PLACE NEW YORK

In the 1870s, when paper could be made much more cheaply from wood pulp rather than cotton rags, and inexpensive full-color printing, chromolithography, became possible at last after the Civil War, the advertising trade card exploded into popularity, with both consumers and merchants.

Ads in newspapers and magazines were still in black and white, but the trade cards, produced in all sizes but most commonly around the size of a modern postcard, were lushly lithographed in color with appealing images well designed and drawn. The backs, imprinted with often florid sales prose, extolled the manufacturer and his product. Generally given out free by merchants in their stores, sometimes as premiums included in the product package, the cards were printed in incredibly large numbers and avidly collected, primarily by women and children to paste in their scrap albums.

Now was the time for Santa to put in his most effective appearance as product salesman—which he did, flogging many kinds of products throughout the 1880s and 1890s, the heyday of the advertising trade card. When the cards lost out to the advertising power of the color-augmented magazines that were rapidly expanding at the end of the century, he promptly put his sales talents to work in the magazine ads.

An 1872 cigar box label. Cigars became popular after the Civil War—General Grant was a noted smoker. Santa appears to be delivering a load of them to grateful gents in the Old West. Here he of course smokes a cigar rather than a pipe. The hunchback Punch figure riding in the back of the sleigh may refer to the famous Cuban cigar brand of the same name.

Macy's department store created a sensation in 1874 when it promoted Christmas gifts to passersby with a spectacular window display of ten thousand dollars' worth of imported dolls. This rare trade card was given away by the store that same Christmas as part of their promotion. A rather gnomelike brown-suited Santa crawls out of the fireplace bringing gifts from the store.

➔ Baldwin the Clothier in New York, specialists in boys' clothing, gave away "Christmas Stories," a thirty-two-page illustrated booklet, to the store's faithful customers in 1874.

CHRISTMAS STORIES.
HOLIDAY GIFT TO THE PATRONS OF THE BOYS' DEPARTMENT.
A VISIT FROM
SANTA CLAUS
FROM BALDWIN THE CLOTHIER

America's great Centennial Exposition was held in Philadelphia in 1876, and for the occasion G. A. Schwarz tied in a promotion of its "Grand Christmas Exhibition" of "Toys, Dolls, Fancy Goods and Novelties" with a full-color card busy with Santa arriving and Father Time tolling the bells.

Santa emerges from the "Bee Hive," apparently the name of a fancy goods store, in 1879. The store's address does not appear anywhere on the card.

Wm. H. Frear, of Troy, New York, was a firm believer of advertising with Santa, taking advantage of the new full-color printing to feature him in a smart blue, red, and green outfit, plus fur trim. And balloons.

A distinct improvement on Santa's appearance from Macy's 1874 card, this yellow-suited Santa promoting Macy's fancy dry goods around 1880 is a full-sized and proper-looking American giftbringer.

This Santa, for Seattle Coal, is another matter—back to a somewhat misshapen dwarf, in brown fur. A modern product for the time, though, instead of old- fashioned logs in the fireplace.

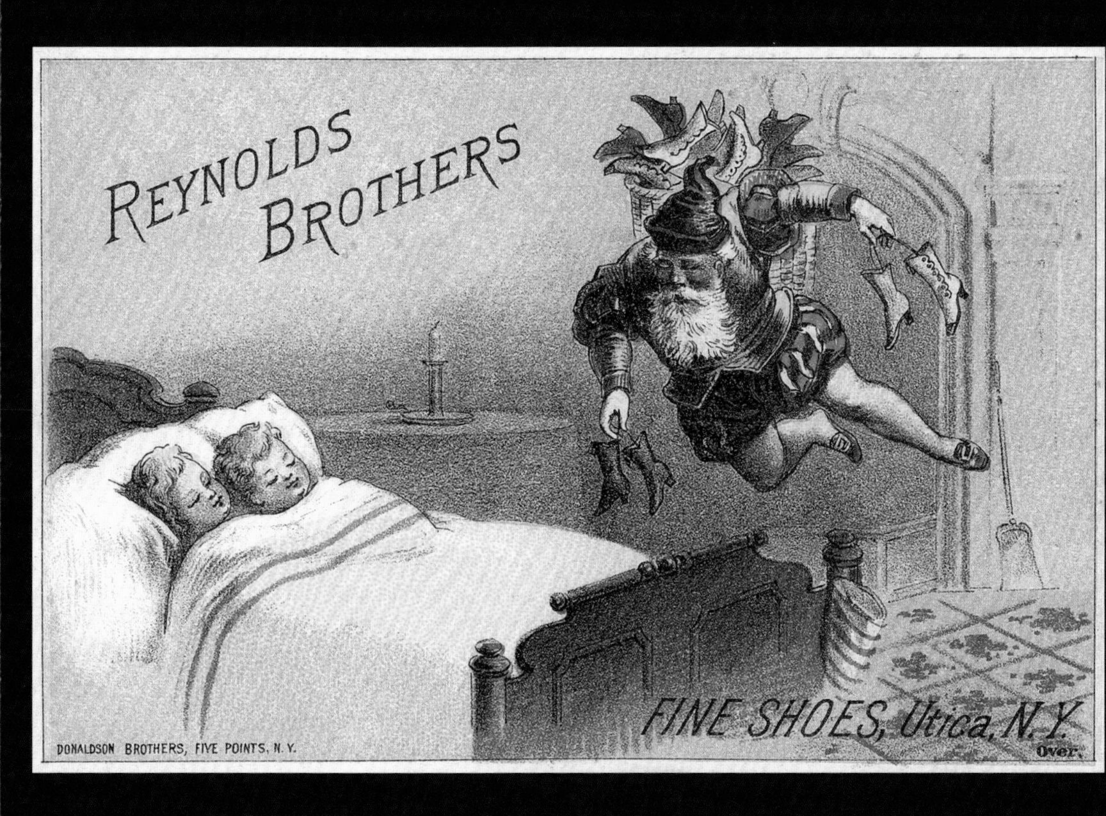

He flies! Without his sleigh or reindeer. Bringing Reynolds Brothers shoes to the little tykes, Santa is imaginatively outfitted in a Renaissance costume of slashed puffed sleeves and slashed breeches, with yellow hose.

You can almost hear the large plum pudding bounce out of the fireplace when it hits bottom. An American variation on the European giftbringer "pick-'em-up" gift delivery.

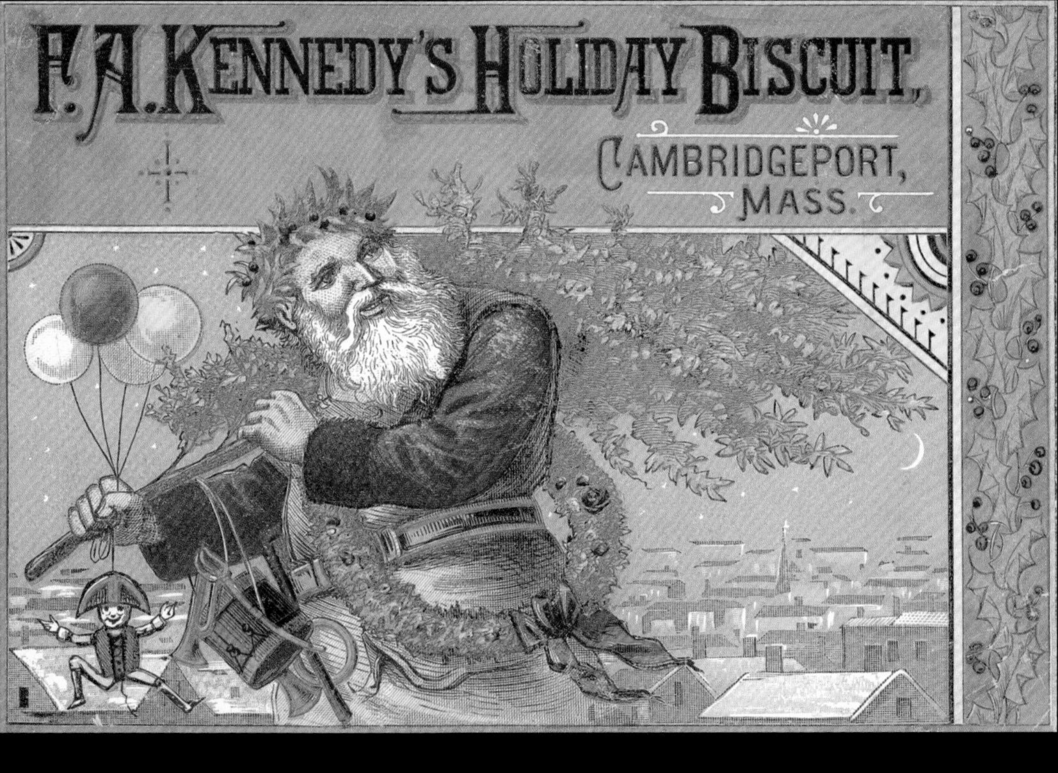

F. A. Kennedy's Holiday Biscuits may have been an English product made in America, since it's Father Christmas, not Santa Claus, who appears on this 1880s label.

Santa plugging Ayer's Cherry Pectoral, a highly successful patent medicine concoction promoted as a cure for "Colds, Coughs, and All Diseases of the Throat and Lungs," on a store counter display from the 1880s. Ayer advertised his nostrum with trade cards showing children happy after using his product. It was later discovered that it contained at least 20 percent ethyl alcohol—and heroin. Santa has a rather sly look to him. Do you suppose he *knows*?

Getting Around

ow did the various giftbringers arrive at people's houses? Where did they come from? Or return to?

The original St. Nicholas, the holy bishop, usually either rode in on a donkey or a white horse or walked from house to house distributing his gifts. In Holland, he and Black Peter arrive by ship from Spain (Black Peter is said to be a Moor). No word as to exactly where in Spain they live. Elsewhere, there is no clear explanation of the saint's abode, the assumption being that he simply appears from Heaven. Krampus, his sometime servant, was clearly from Hell.

The other European giftbringers—Father Christmas, Père Nöel, Weihnachtsmann, et al.—either walked, rode, or were pulled by a fine variety of steeds: horses, goats, donkeys, polar bears, the occasional moose, and, of course, a reindeer or two, up to the full complement of twelve. As magical folk figures, they simply arrived and departed mysteriously in the cold winter night on Christmas Eve.

This kind of thinking was ultimately not satisfying to Americans. Washington Irving's 1809 Dutch St. Nicholas flew through the sky in a wagon pulled by a horse, while the jolly old elf in Clement Moore's 1822 poem arrived and departed in a sleigh pulled by eight tiny reindeer. But

still—from where and back to where?

Thomas Nast, the imaginative and gifted artist famous for his series of illustrations of Santa Claus and his doings in *Harper's Weekly*, finally came to grips with this problem. He decided that Santa Claus lived at the North Pole. In an 1882 illustration of Santa sitting on a "Christmas Box" talking to children, Nast put the sender's address on the box as "St. Nicholas, North Pole." He was likely building on Santa's image of being clad in a fur suit and traveling in a sleigh pulled by reindeer as described in Moore's poem. The North Pole had also been the destination of several (unsuccessful) arctic expeditions beginning in 1818 and continuing into the 1850s, heightening the public's fascination with the place. It appeared to Nast to be the ideal remote location for Santa to set up shop, equidistant to most places on the globe for his travels. Now everyone knew where Santa lived.

But real-life travel in the United States was rapidly changing: the transcontinental railroad connected the nation coast-to-coast in 1869; the automobile was invented in 1885; the bicycle was perfected around 1890; the dirigible in 1900; and the Wright brothers' airplane was flown in 1903. Santa found he had to keep up with the times when it came to his transportation. Soon he was seen arriving in fanciful flying contraptions, then by balloon, dirigible, and airplane; on land by train, bicycle, and automobile; on water by motorboat. He prided himself on being up to date.

The giftbringer in Europe sometimes was made to look much like a tramp, peddler, beggar, or rag picker, patches on his sack and clothes, trudging along with his walking stick. This folk idea may have come from the nearness of Christmas to the end of the year—a tired old man nearing the end of his travels. This postcard was printed in Saxony and postmarked 1909 in Michigan.

Checking the signpost. The idea of Santa walking down roads from house to house had to be a novelty to Americans in 1906, which may have been the appeal of this postcard printed in Germany, mailed to West Sand Lake, New York.

A poignant conception of the giftbringer continuing his lonely way to the next house.

German postcard artists began to think of other ways for the pedestrian giftbringer to make his journey more quickly—and more interestingly. This card was mailed from Passaic, New Jersey, in 1907.

Reindeer pulled Santa's sleigh. In America, that was settled. In Europe, it most definitely was not. A number of different animals were brought in to pull the sleigh (at least the sleigh was agreed upon), including, but by no means limited to, a goat, donkey, moose, and horse, as illustrated in this scrap picture of the 1890s.

It is odd to see a Father Christmas figure using a goat to help carry the gifts, as in the West the goat is considered a symbol of Satan. Or perhaps we're meant to make an association with the Norse god Thor's two goats, which pulled his chariot. On the other hand, sometimes a goat is just a goat.

Father Christmas arriving on a white charger in the style of a fifteenth-century Italian Renaissance equestrian figure. St. Nicholas traditionally rode a white horse, but nothing this grand.

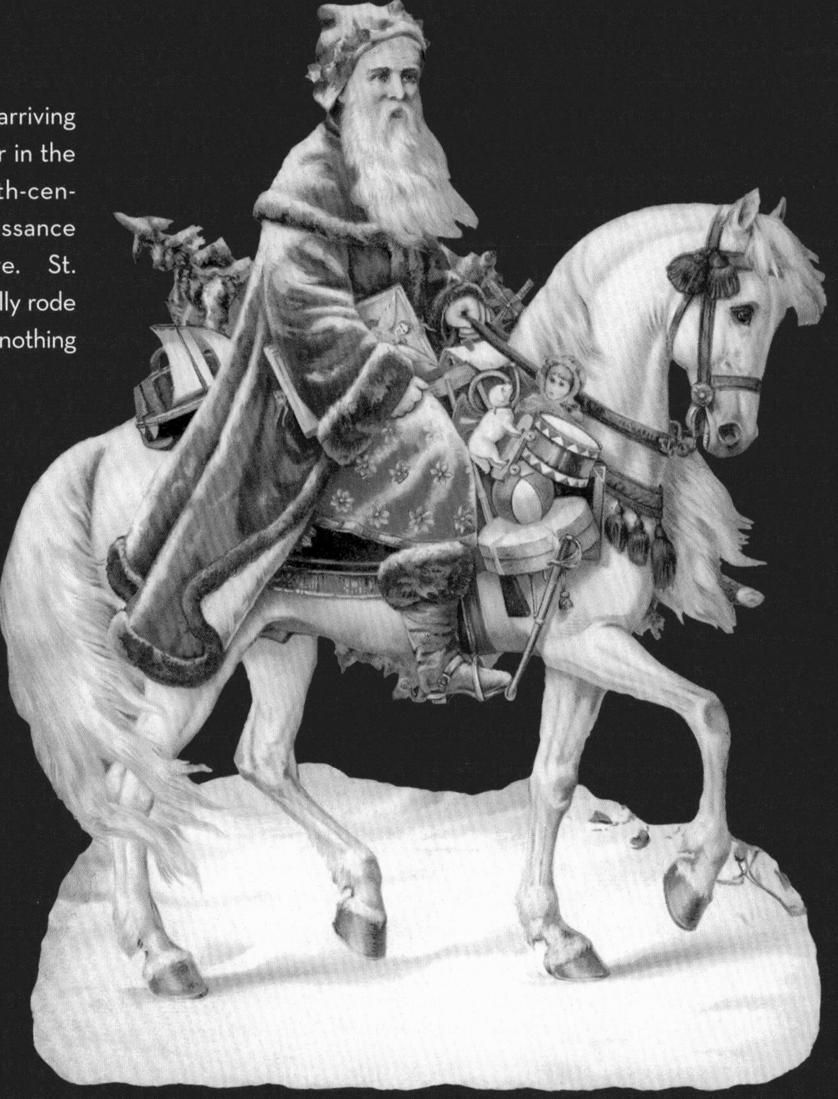

A merry Father Christmas jingles and jangles along, holding the reins and switches, riding a spirited donkey with not a sleigh in sight.

← The Santa Express, in an English scrap picture of the late 1890s; the locomotive is an 1860s London and North Western Railway model, adding a little nostalgia for even earlier days. Still, the idea was to show the gift-bringer being up to date using modern technology for his Christmas Eve arrival. The engineer should be a holly-crowned Father Christmas, but he looks more like Santa—possibly a concession to the American market and its importation of great quantities of English scrap pictures.

→ Another up-to-date Santa, from 1894, this time flying a kind of bat-plane contraption. He is somehow steering it at a right angle to the presumed flight direction, but this is nine years before the Wright brothers flew an airplane that actually worked. Before then, artists could concoct whatever they could imagine as a flying machine, and did. The caption below this cartoon by Frederick Opper for the humor magazine *Puck* reads, "Even Santa Claus's reindeer will have to give way to something newer before long."

➛ The reindeer are gone. Santa is dropping off gifts from a French 1908 Voisin biplane on a 1913 postcard printed in Germany.

➛ A late-1920s po card has Santa dumpi gifts like propagan leaflets.

➤ The Weihnachstmann is on his way with gifts and boxes of cigars after landing in a dirigible on this cigar box label printed in Germany around 1905. From the department of oversights and missed promotional opportunities: he is smoking a pipe, not a cigar.

➤ When the safety bicycle featuring equal-sized wheels, a diamond frame, and rear-chain drive was perfected around 1890, the bicycling craze was on, enjoyed by all classes and both sexes. Santa found one convenient too, confirmed on this cigar box label from 1900.

Now serving island dwellers.

→ Chugging through the night in an automobile around 1905, the giftbringer enjoys the services of a driver.

← Drive-by gift delivery in a flying 1908 auto driven by a dyspeptic dwarf.

Other Santa Escapades

oward the end of the nineteenth century and the beginning of the twentieth, a certain ennui seemed to set in with artists and writers about the sameness of Santa's seasonal activities: arriving by one means or another, going down the chimney, filling the stockings, leaving the gifts or handing them out, blessing the good children, chastising the bad, then up the chimney or out the door and away.

So now and then, for a little variety, artists would show a few mishaps in the course of Santa's rounds: his sleigh overturned, tripped up by mischievous boys, or attacked by mutinous toys. It turns out Santa also had an eye for the ladies. Don't tell Mrs. Claus.

Another artistic conceit was to show him in the guise of a mailman, or a chef, or Uncle Sam. The possibilities were endless.

And then there was politics and social commentary for Santa to get involved in. A unique American humor magazine, *Puck*, was started by a cartoonist, Joseph Keppler, in 1877, and lasted until 1918. *Puck* featured mostly political and social satire in drawings by Keppler, later by others, from a Democratic point of view—Grover Cleveland was the magazine's political hero. It was the first weekly publication to successfully use full-color lithography, and it wasn't long before Santa appeared in the color

Santa experiences runner failure on his way to give a talk to children in the 1886 children's book *Santa Claus' Visit to the Schoolroom*. He's also short a few reindeer.

double-page centerfold to express his opinions on political and social issues.

Defecting artists from *Puck* founded the competitor humor magazine *Judge* in 1881. Under later editorial leadership, *Judge* became allied with the Republican Party, attacking the Democratic administration of Grover Cleveland and supporting the presidential candidacy of William McKinley. Sure enough, Santa appeared in its December 27, 1887, color spread as Uncle Sam, the "National Santa Claus," surrounded by a constellation of political figures—most now long forgotten—as politically symbolic toys.

By the 1880s, the world had changed so much that Santa felt he'd better read up on modern times so he could stay relevant: the telephone was invented in 1876, the phonograph in 1877, the incandescent light in 1879, the radio in 1896. He was no longer an elf and was by then portrayed as a full-size person living in the real world. Artists delighted in the opportunities for showing him using the new technologies as part of his operations.

The world was also getting bigger—or at least Americans were becoming more aware of just how big it was, now that a nationwide railroad system allowed people and goods to be transported to the far corners of the country, or by huge steamships to other continents. McLoughlin Bros., a large and famous American publisher of children's books and games, responded to the growing interest in the world at large by issuing a fine new full-color Christmas book for children in 1881, *Around the World with Santa-Claus*. After visiting different countries and their Christmas customs, all elaborately illustrated, Santa takes a canoe ride in the Wild West to smoke a peace pipe with an Indian chief. The benevolence and goodwill Santa brought was offset by events in the real world: 1881 was also the year the great Sioux chief Sitting Bull finally surrendered to the army, the Indians having all but lost their struggle to remain free.

A larger worldview was also likely causing children to ask parents awkward questions like, "How can Santa be in all those countries on Christmas Eve?" and "How can Santa be both in Macy's and Gimbels at the same time?"

SUPPLEMENT TO THE New York World, Sunday, Dec. 16, 1900
Geo. W. Peck,
CHRISTMAS
The World
FUNNY SIDE
Editor.
1900 COPYRIGHT, BY THE PRESS PUB. CO. N.Y.
The Mutiny of the Toys.
"We refuse to be given to a lot of Terrible Children Who would only destroy us!"

It was already happening by 1900: the American economy was churning out such an abundance of toys that kids considered them expendable—there was always more to be had from the good and generous Santa. From the eight-page Sunday supplement to Joseph Pulitzer's *New York World*, December 16, 1900.

The giftbringer arrives as the postman.

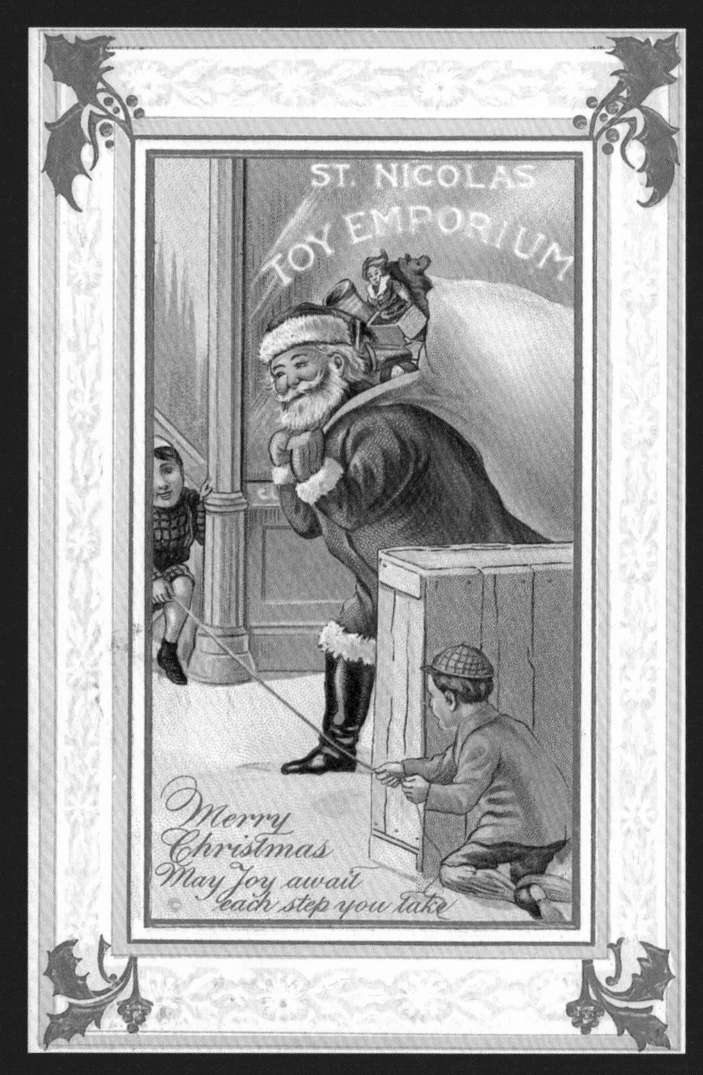

→ Santa may rethink the matter and start bringing switches again if the two little jokers succeed in tripping him up. An American postcard from 1911.

The giftbringer as chef, with quite a bit of the Old Father Christmas about him—Father of the Feast, drinking, merriment, and all that.

← He's really just checking to see how she likes the lingerie he brought.

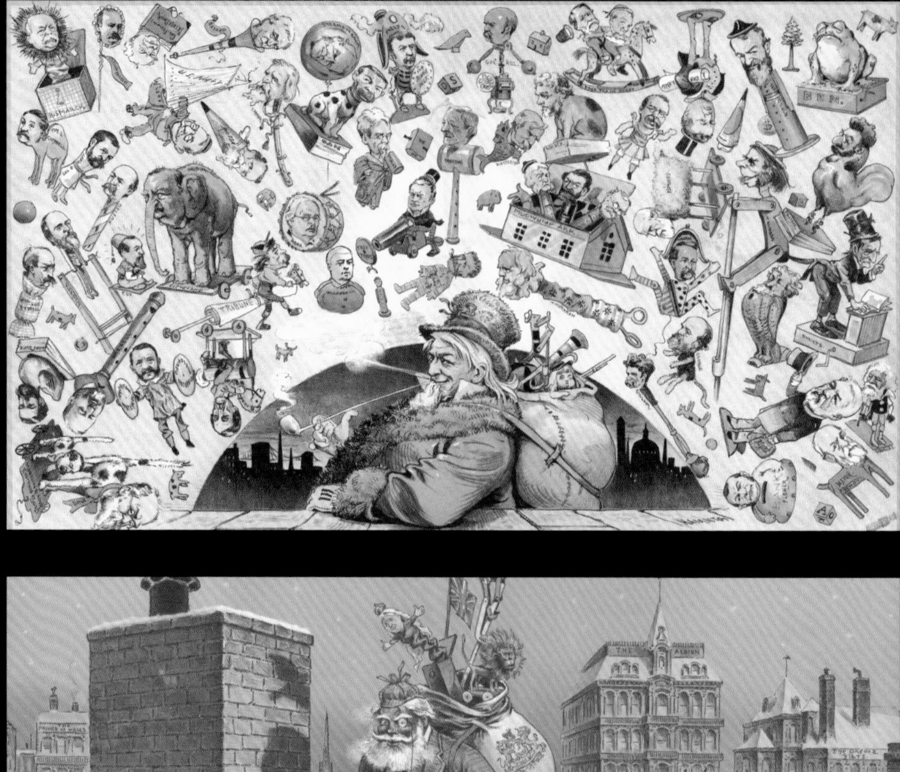
TRIBUNE
B.E.M.

THE
ALBION

"Well, they don't seem to have much use for me! They're like a lot of little old men and women! If they are going to get like this, I may as well retire from the business!" *Puck* cartoonist Frederick Opper comments on Christmas in juvenile high society during the Gilded Age of the 1890s.

➤ "The National Santa Claus" surrounded by a nimbus of toy politicians and other toy movers and shakers of the day—all men—as satirical gifts to the nation. Some of them are still recognizable today.

➤ "English You Know." Father Christmas is updated by cartoonist Frederick Opper in the American humor magazine *Puck* as a British Santa Claus. The Queen Victoria jumping jack would probably have elicited her famous comment again: "We are not amused." The reindeer, of course, wear monocles.

Uncle Sam Claus. A German postcard import postmarked Thomas, Michigan, 1914. An earlier 1905 version of the same figure was a blue-robed Weihnachtsmann, but here he's being suited up as Uncle Sam to appeal to American patriotism. Three years later, in 1917, during World War I, the United States declared war against Germany.

Weinachtsmann pauses in the forest to make a phone call, checking if an address in his little red book is correct. The hare thinks it's hilarious.

Santa takes a break to catch up on the latest issue of *Modern Age*, a literary magazine of the 1880s published in New York.

Smoking a peace pipe with an Indian chief, Santa has gone native and is wearing moccasins for the occasion. An illustration from the children's book *Around the World with Santa-Claus*, published in 1881 by McLoughlin Bros., New York.

Fantasy and Fairy Folklore

hile much about Christmas has always been mystical, magical, and fantastic, including, or perhaps especially, the giftbringers, leave it to the Victorians to up the ante. They thrilled to tales of ghosts—Charles Dickens's (1812–1870) famous and familiar Christmas story from 1843, *A Christmas Carol*, was subtitled *A Ghost Story of Christmas*—and many believed, or wanted to believe, in fairies, goblins, and elves.

The belief in a magical, mostly invisible world of tiny beings inhabiting the natural world was not unique to the British Isles; it was common throughout Europe and many other parts of the world. Fairies and elves were believed to be unpredictable, capable of both helping humans by bringing gifts for children and breaking evil spells, and, conversely, ruining crops, causing accidents, or even stealing human children. Spirits of all kinds were thought to be particularly active during the Twelve Days of Christmas when they haunted the long, dark nights.

But it was in Ireland and the British Isles that the fairy kingdom truly flourished. Between 1840 and 1870, a golden age of fairy painting was created by painters responding to the urgent desire of Victorians to escape from their world of materialism and scientific rigor into one of magic and wonder. As the exchange of Christmas cards became increasingly popular

from the 1870s on, it seemed natural that fairies and elves should also be represented on them as part of the Christmas season. By then, much of the threatening or ghoulish elements had disappeared from fairy imagery, replaced by the playful and sentimental.

Elves were viewed in the Scandinavian countries as mischievous little beings that lived in the attic, or under the floorboards, or in the barn. At Christmastime, they required a bowl of rice pudding to be left out for them, or there would be trouble at the old homestead. In England, elves were part of fairyland, dancing in moonlit meadows with other magical creatures. In America, elves were employed throughout the year as Santa's workforce at his North Pole manufactory hand making toys for his Christmas Eve deliveries. While not the originator of this idea, Thomas Nast popularized it so thoroughly through his series of Santa illustrations for *Harper's Weekly* that working elves became forever after part of Santa's operations.

A further expression of the Victorian delight in the fantastic was giving food and inanimate objects human attributes and actions. Later, around the turn of the twentieth century, this resulted in such delightful representations as an animated Christmas tree and a snowman family out for a stroll.

Anthropomorphic edibles like these printed in 1881 were a favorite English fantasy associated with the original feasting, drinking, and merriment of the season.

This boiling pot appears as a medieval imp from the fires of Hell.

➔ An excited Father Christmas dubs "Sir Loin" while the other main courses look on in this 1870s card.

➔ As in a magic dark incantation, Santa rises out of a huge steaming plum pudding surrounded by dancing red imps. A greeting card conjuration by L. Prang & Co., Boston, from 1885.

A
MERRY CHRISTMAS
AND
A HAPPY NEW YEAR

May Santa Claus bring Joy and Pleasure
To thee and thine in Fullest Measure!

A MERRY
CHRISTMAS

➤ German pine cone gnomes start the festivities. Postmarked Denver, Colorado, 1908.

➤ "In this Landscape you can trace, A Jolly Father Christmas face." Pictorial illusionism in the 1870s.

➤ A small angel has the ear of a winter spirit wreathed in mistletoe. This 1908 postcard image may be a vestige of very old pagan and medieval beliefs in a winter solstice figure known as the Green Man, an embodiment of all green and growing things who symbolized the new life of spring emerging from the death of winter.

An ambulatory Christmas tree lights up with the giftbringer.

Tree greets snowman on a 1909 postcard mailed in Iowa.

A snowman family out for an evening stroll in 1910.

A winter spirit as a fat, jolly snowman on his way as the giftbringer, ready with his magic wand to make all Christmas wishes come true. His dwarf driver appears a little perplexed about the whole thing, and so does one of the deer. A unique Christmas Eve vision from Germany, postmarked at Poughkeepsie, New York, around 1910.

Elves hauling in the yule log harassed by goblins, from the 1870s. A tradition going back to pagan and medieval times, involving many superstitions, the yule log was to be kept burning during the Twelve Days of Christmas, lit from a fragment of the previous year's log. If the fire went out, the household would have bad luck during the coming year. In order to keep the log burning for so many days, some used actual tree trunks, with one end sticking out into the room. As fireplaces shrank in size, so did the logs, until the custom disappeared altogether.

Fairy witches brewing trouble in fairyland, 1870s.

A fairy dance over a meadow stream, 1878.

A Joyful Christmas to

← Young barn owls being teased and tormented by fairies, around 1885. Animals, especially birds, have always been part of the fairy world, but were not always pictured as well treated.

← Frost fairies do battle on an 1884 greeting card by L. Prang & Co., Boston. The Christmas greeting has inadvertently been printed upside down.

→ A baby flower fairy, around 1885. As the years went by, fairies were pictured increasingly as sweet and innocent, in real contrast to the menacing world sometimes created by the early fairy painters.

A pretty fairy child astride a butterfly made perfect sense for a Christmas greeting in England in the late 1880s given the English love of all things fairyland. John George Naish (1824-1905) first painted fairies riding moths and butterflies in the 1850s. Late-Victorian sentimentalism converted the traditionally mischievous fairy into the idealized cherubic Victorian child.

Christmas Characters

he Christmas giftbringers changed costumes, names, companions, appearances, accessories, and roles, yet they endured over the years, even centuries. But there was another, secondary tier of folk figures that appeared only for a time, played their role, then for the most part disappeared, except the characters in the English popular theater of the pantomime.

An English Christmas card of the 1870s, originally mounted in an American album, presented the unique figure of "Mother Christmas"—a sort of fairy witch figure apparently conceived as a counterpart to Father Christmas. She clearly did not make it into the permanent pantheon of Christmas folk figures. Other odd conceptions include a Chinese Father Christmas and a grotesque life- size St. Nicholas nutcracker.

Winter itself became personified in folklore as a figure in a snowy white robe with icicles for his hair and beard. "King Winter," whose associate was Jack Frost, wore a crown of icicles as well as an icicle beard, as portrayed in the 1870s. In his brief appearance in the lore of Christmas, King Winter served in the role of giftbringer, rewarding the good children with sweets and toys, the bad with birch rods. Father Christmas, Père Nöel, Weihnachtsmann, and Santa Claus soon put him out of business.

For a time, from the 1880s to the early twentieth century, black minstrel

A menacing nutcracker St. Nicholas comes to gaping life brandishing a wicked bundle of switches. Oddly, instead of running for their lives, the children dance joyfully around the ogre. From a German postcard distributed in France around 1905.

figures were popular on Christmas cards, probably considered part of the "merry" and "happy" aspect of the season. These of course were images of black people created by white people—racial caricatures that were demeaning to African Americans, portraying them as musically talented but otherwise no more than entertaining clowns.

Minstrelsy was originally based on the performances of talented slave dancers, comedians, and musicians on southern plantations. Christmas celebrations in the slave quarters sometimes lasted as many as three to six days, encouraged by slaveholders who thought they might serve as a sort of safety valve, placating the slaves for another year of oppression. There was much singing and dancing accompanied by fiddles, banjos (a true black instrument, brought over from Africa), triangles, bones, tambourines, and drums.

All this was appropriated as a source of theatrical material by white performers in blackface who first entertained audiences with great success in 1829 and 1830. After the Civil War, white minstrelsy became less popular, and black minstrelsy more so. Minstrelsy was the dominant form of entertainment in America for more than sixty years.

An especially popular minstrel stereotype on the Christmas cards of the period was the "zip coon," a Northern urban black dandy who reveled in flashy clothes, doing new dances, courting the ladies, showing off, and having a good time. And, on one card, he's wishing the recipient "A Right Merrie Christmas." Many of these cards were designed in England, where minstrelsy was also very popular.

In 1881, a large Christmas card was created by the hugely successful Boston lithographer L. Prang & Company, featuring a tall black man as "A Modern Santa Claus" to promote their line of Christmas cards. Clearly intended to be a humorous variation of the zip coon for the amusement of white folk at Christmastime, this is a remarkably rare conception of the giftbringer.

The scheduling of Christmas very near the end of the year sometimes introduced another folk figure—Father Time—into the seasonal festivities. A thin old man, gaunt with a long white beard, he looked somewhat like Father Christmas, except he had wings ("time flies"). The two were acquaintances, it seems, Father Time even helping out with the gift giving.

The ancestor of pantomime, a traditional English theatrical form of entertainment, was the Italian commedia dell'arte, a sort of improvised burlesque comedy very much intended for adults, imported to England but popular throughout Europe in the sixteenth century.

The main characters were Pantaloon, a scheming old buffoon;

Graziano, a pompous professor; Harlequin, a scamp; Colombine, a simple young woman; and Punch, a slow-witted hunchback. Stage antics involved masks, miming, exaggerated gestures, dancing, music, tumbling, and limited dialogue. In eighteenth-century England, the art form was modified to highlight the roguish Harlequin and his romance with Columbine, with the addition of many special effects and lavish costuming, and became known as harlequinade.

What came to be known as pantomime evolved out of harlequinade in the early nineteenth century—same colorful circus spectacle, but with the clown replacing Harlequin in importance. The most famous clown was Joseph Grimaldi (1779–1837), whose creation of "Joey the Clown" made him a pantomime star and the clown a fixture of the English Christmas.

Pantomime became associated with Christmas in the 1830s and 1840s, when some of its wilder elements were edited out to be more acceptable for the entertainment of children during the season. The commedia dell'arte characters were replaced with retellings of fairy tales, myths, and fables, by wretched puns, extravagant spectacles, shouted exchanges between the actors and the audience, cross-dressing among the characters (always a big hit), and references to current events. The children loved it. But so did their parents. They all flocked to the performances, which opened on December 26, Boxing Day, and ran through the Twelve Days of Christmas.

For some reason, pantomine did not cross over to America, despite the high percentage of English people in the population from the very beginnings of the country. Perhaps the strong Puritan influence may have had something to do with it; celebrations at Christmas of any kind were banned in the New England states for many years. This attitude gradually softened as people in the other states embraced the holiday as a family celebration, until finally, on June 26, 1870, Congress declared Christmas a national holiday.

Mother Christmas comes with a magic wand, looking like the good witch in seventeenth-century garb, with a little Mother Goose thrown in. Presumably a counterpart to Father Christmas, she was not seen again after her appearance on this 1870s greeting card.

Father Christmas as Chinese emperor. A second look reveals that the low bows of the two courtiers are anatomically impossible. This English card was created in the 1870s, one of the high

King Winter, a short-lived German personification of winter who brings gifts to children with Jack Frost as his helper, as told in a children's book from the 1870s.

The English version of a similar winter character, also from the 1870s, clothed in icicles and looking a little fierce.

"The King of the Holly" on this English greeting card from around 1885 can be traced back to the fifteenth century and the personification of holly as "king" and ivy as "queen." Folklore considered holly, with its sharp prickly leaves, as male, and the smoother, clinging ivy as female. English medieval and Renaissance songs often cast a rivalry between holly and ivy as a version of the battle of the sexes.

Winter relaxes with his pipe while keeping a wary eye on the raven, the bird of ill omen, on this postcard printed in Germany, post-marked Chicago, Illinois, 1910.

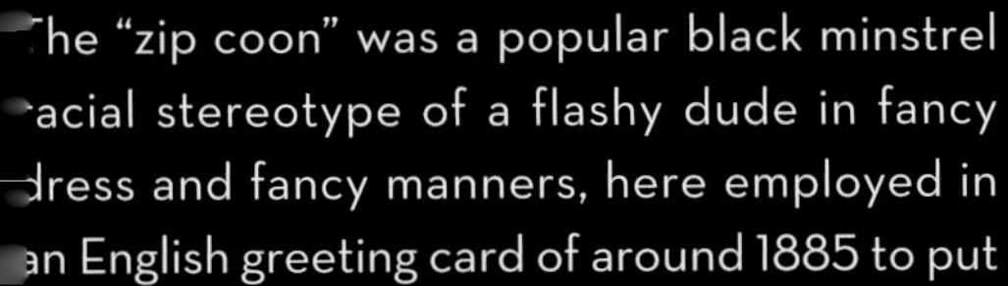

The "zip coon" was a popular black minstrel racial stereotype of a flashy dude in fancy dress and fancy manners, here employed in an English greeting card of around 1885 to put

A black child playing the banjo while riding a high-wheeler bicycle dressed as a clown seemed ideal for conveying "Jolly Christmas" wishes to white folks in 1883.

More black minstrel Christmas merrymakers claimed to be trouble free, jolly, and singing their cheery song the whole day long on a card from the 1890s.

"A Modern Santa Claus." Smartly dressed in a long coat richly trimmed in fur with a large hat, a stereotypical black Northern urban dandy has arrived in a coach as the giftbringer. The artist, undoubtedly white, of this 1881 greeting card produced by L. Prang & Co., Boston, to promote its line of Christmas cards, mockingly shows toys being held upside down and the large front wheel of a high-wheeler bicycle positioned as a saint's halo.

Father Time brings the gifts, Father Christmas checks his list, the children gather expectantly in the 1890s.

⤎ Father Time introduces Father Christmas, in a monk's robe, to a jester, or Lord of Misrule, who presided over the Christmas festivities of feasts, dancing, mumming, music, masques, and madcap merrymaking in medieval times.

A performance of British Christmas pantomime illustrated in an English children's book from the 1890s. Joey the Clown was a new character created by actor Joseph Grimaldi in the early 1800s. Columbine and Harlequin, original sixteenth-century Italian commedia dell'arte characters, continue to entertain.

➤ Joey the Clown was forever getting in trouble with the law. His voluminous pockets are stuffed with stolen comestibles for his Christmas feast. From an 1887 English scrapbook.

➤ Pantaloon (or Pantalone), an original commedia dell'arte character portrayed as a foolish old man, sometimes rich, sometimes poor, but always being duped by someone, became a stock character in British Christmas pantomime as the butt of Clown's jokes. Clown runs him down with a perambulator, two babies still in it, the mother aghast nearby, in a scene that was apparently hilarious to people in 1887.

← Father Christmas reviews a parade of pantomime characters—Clown, Pantaloon, Columbine, and Harlequin—in this 1880s card.

→ Clown is not all bad. In a series of Christmas greeting cards from the 1880s, he becomes Everyman's friend and defender by playing tricks on dishonest tradesmen and other cheaters. The dairyman who dilutes his milk with water and chalk gets doused with his own bogus product.

A Creature Christmas

lthough nowhere in the Gospel Infancy Narratives of Matthew and Luke are animals described as being present at the birth of Jesus, people in the Middle Ages believed that to be an oversight and filled in a few blanks. Since then, a long list of animals have been associated with Christmas. Legends sprang up that a donkey carried Mary to Bethlehem; the donkey and the ox knelt before the child; the rooster crowed, announcing the birth; the robin singed its breast red from being too close to the flames while beating its wings to keep the fire alive; the stork tore out its feathers to make a soft bed for the newborn (becoming ever after the patron of babies); and a host of other animals are said to have been at the Nativity.

Later European legends claimed that at midnight on Christmas Eve, oxen knelt in their stables, barnyard animals could speak, and bees sang psalms and hymns, all in honor of Jesus' birth.

People in the Victorian age took this a bit further by having all kinds of animals celebrating the season, acting like humans. Human-acting, or anthropomorphic, animals is a very old idea. A three-thousand-year-old Egyptian papyrus is illustrated with a lion and an antelope playing a board game. Bugs acting like people, though, was an entirely new twist in the

Santa conducts a dance of the animals in celebration of the 1892 Christmas season.

Christmas celebration. Perhaps bugs were thought of as just another part of the fairy world that had been so popular in painting and illustration in England at the time.

The idea of animals dressed in human clothes, yet another old tradition, was brought to perfection in the nineteenth century through the rich illustrative possibilities of the new full-color lithography. Images of cute dogs and cats abounded in all sorts of frocks in all sorts of situations, as might be expected, but other, more unusual animals were also found disporting themselves in handsome threads.

And then there is the matter of dead birds—on their backs, their little curled feet in the air—pictured on Christmas cards with greetings like, "May Yours be a Joyful Christmas" and "A Loving Christmas Greeting." These are real head-scratchers, and all explanations are only speculations, as there is no known documentation of their meaning. Christmas card historians offer only that the Victorians were a thoroughly sentimental lot and that the cards were popular. Death at a young age was common then and highly sentimentalized; a small dead bird may have represented a loving memory. But why bring this up at Christmas?

Grasshopper musicians practicing the "Hop Waltz" on an 1881 greeting card.

Crickets on the hearth dance around a mini yule log in this 1870s card.

Bug poker. Possibly a little friendly after-Christmas dinner game. Insects were frequently painted as part of the fairy kingdom in England, later joining fairies as Christmas card subjects.

On this card from the 1880s, a bug couple in love read the French romantic novel *Paul & Virginia*, written by Jacques Henri Bernardin in 1788, translated into English and widely read in Victorian England. In the story, Virginia drowns at sea and Paul dies broken-hearted—very appealing to Victorian sentimentality. There is the unexplained matter, though, of the menacing moth behind the couple in the picture wielding a large sword over their heads, and about to swing.

Creepy-crawly Christmas. The barely readable legend in the bottom left-hand corner of this 1870s card reads, "The evening return, ants and their cattle," providing a nature lesson as well as a greeting. The artist may never have seen an actual aphid.

Christmas dinner in the 1870s.

Making a joyous noise in the 1880s.

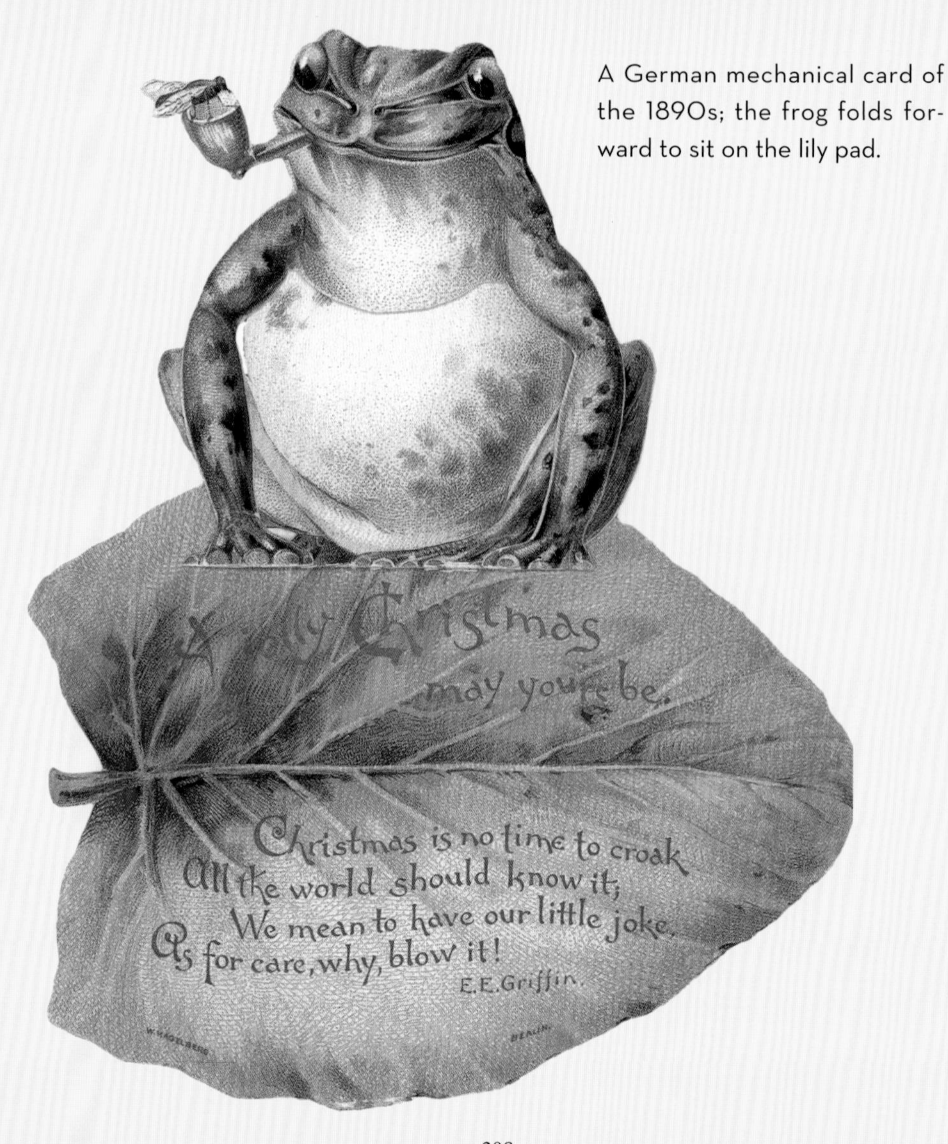

A German mechanical card of the 1890s; the frog folds forward to sit on the lily pad.

A Bouquet for Goldilocks? Fangs and claws are all agleam in this large dark card proclaiming "Though bare the fields and wintry storm, This bear bears CHRISTMAS greetings warm." Published by L. Prang & Co., Boston, around 1885.

Celebrating the season at the local rodent tavern in the 1870s.

THE KINDLY ROBIN.

Castell Brothers.

Nº 520
PRINTED IN BAVARIA.

Copyright.

CHRISTMAS
For a fish on frolic bent,
Christmas is the element!

Ballerina Mademoiselle Puss on pointe in her Christmas performance in the 1890s.

"May yours be a Joyful Christmas." A dead European robin frozen from the cold was bound to elicit Victorian sympathy and pity and may reference common stories of poor children freezing to death at Christmas. The 1880s card may have invoked one's own good fortune and that of the card's recipient during the holidays.

"A Loving Christmas Greeting." Another dead bird, likely a wren. The robin and the wren were considered in British and Irish folk-

NOTES ON THE EPHEMERA

Unless otherwise noted, all antique paper ephemera and prints reproduced in this book were printed by the nineteenth-century color process of chromolithography, and are from The John Grossman Collection of Antique Images.

Cover: Greeting card; L. Prang & Co., Boston; 1885. **End papers:** Uncut sheet, Weihnachtsmann puppets; 13$\frac{3}{8}$"h x 16$\frac{3}{8}$"w; Gustav Rühn, Neuruppin, Germany; c1870s. **Page 2:** Greeting card; 5$\frac{3}{4}$"h x 5$\frac{3}{4}$"w; gilded; England; c1885. **Page 6:** Postcard; embossed; Germany; postmarked Poughkeepsie, N.Y.; c1912. **Page 224:** Mechanical greeting card (Punch and Toby); book hinges forward; die cut; Raphael Tuck & Sons, Ltd.; designed in London, printed in Germany; c1900.

CHRISTMAS AS YOU'VE NEVER KNOWN IT

Page 9: Greeting card; B. Bros., London, England; c1885. **Page 10, 11, 20:** Greeting card; England; c1895. **Page 13:** Greeting card; B. Bros., London, England; c1885. **Page 14:** Greeting card (old couple at window); die-cut window opening; F. E. Weatherby, verse; Hildesheimer & Faulkner; designed in England, printed in Germany; c1890. **Page 14:** Greeting card (couple pouring water on musicians); back of previous card; die-cut window opening; Hildesheimer & Faulkner; designed in England, printed in Germany; c1890. **Page 15:** Greeting card; De La Rue & Co., London, England; inscribed on back, "Dec/77" (1877). **Page 16:** Greeting card; embossed, die cut; R. Canton, London, England; c1870. **Page 17:** Greeting card; verse on back by Frederick Longbridge; Raphael Tuck & Sons, London, England; c1885. **Page 18:** Greeting card; De La Rue & Co., London, England; c1885.

THE SAINTED GIFTBRINGER

Page 23: Postcard; embossed; Paul Finkenrath, Germany; postmarked Barryville, N.Y., 1910. **Page 25:** Scrap; embossed, die cut; Germany; c1890. **Page 26:** Broadside (St. Nicholas); first annual celebration of the Festival of St. Nicholas by the New-York Historical Society; 11$\frac{1}{4}$"h x 7$\frac{1}{2}$"w; commissioned by John Pintard; wood engraving; Alexander Anderson, engraver; letterpress; 1810. *Collection of The New-York Historical Society*. **Page 28:** Postcard (boy putting his boots out for St. Nicholas); embossed; Paul Finkenrath, Germany; postmarked Redding, Cal., 1905. **Page 28:** Postcard (St. Nicholas bringing gifts for adults), embossed; Germany; c1905. **Page 29:** Postcard (St. Nicholas presenting female doll to man); embossed; Germany; c1905. **Page 29:** Postcard (St. Nicholas presenting male doll to woman); embossed; Germany; postmarked in France, 1905. **Page 30:** Postcard; greeting in Dutch; gold stamped; Germany; c1905. **Page 32:** Scrap; embossed, die cut; Littauer & Boysen, Berlin, Germany; c1900. **Page 33:** Postcard; Rafael Neuber, Vienna, Austria; c1900. **Page 34:** Scrap; embossed, die cut; Germany; c1920.

WHEN THE DEVIL CAME TO CHRISTMAS

Page 37,43: Postcard; Austria; c1905. **Page 38:** Scrap; embossed, die cut; Germany; c1890. **Page 39:** Scrap;

embossed, die cut; Germany; c1900. **Page 40:** Postcard; Albert Berger, Vienna, Austria; postmarked Vienna, 1899. **Page 41:** Children's book illustration; *Around the World with Santa-Claus*; 10"h x 7¼"w; R. André, artist; McLoughlin Bros., New York; 1881. **Page 42:** Postcard (Krampus grasping boy); embossed; Illustrated Postal Card Co., New York-Germany; c1910. **Page 42:** Postcard (man and woman puppets of Krampus); embossed; Austria; c1905. **Page 43:** Postcard (Krampus at the pit of Hell); Austria; c1909. **Page 44:** Postcard; greeting in Czechoslovakian; c1905. **Page 45:** Postcard; embossed; Austria; c1900. **Page 46:** Postcard; c1900.

SANTA, WE HARDLY KNOW YE

Page 49: Children's book illustration, *The Children's Friend*; hand-colored lithograph; author and artist unknown; William R. Gilley, New York; 1821. *Courtesy of The American Antiquarian Society.* **Page 50, 62:** Stock advertising give-away (grotesque dwarf-like Santa); 11⅝"h x 7½"w; die cut; c1880. **Page 54:** Weekly newspaper illustration; *New York Mirror*; 5½"h x 9"w; wood engraving; R. Roberts, engraver; January 2, 1841. **Page 55:** Illustration, "Santa Claus. The Night Before New Year"; *New York Mirror*; engraved by Sherman & Smith; 1844. **Page 55:** Sheet music, *Santa Claus Quadrilles*; 13"h x 10"w; b&w lithograph; Harvey B. Dodworth, arranger; Spoodlyks, artist; Firth, Hall & Pond, publishers, New York; G & W Endicott, lithographers, New York; 1846. **Page 56:** Greeting card; 7"h x 8¼"w; Robert Weir, artist (based on his 1846 painting); poem "Visit of St. Nicholas" printed on back; Buek & Lindner, Lithographers, New York; 1884. **Page 57:** Book illustration; *A Visit from St. Nicholas*; Clement C. Moore, LL.D; wood engraving; Theodore Boyd, engraver; Henry M. Onderdonk, New York; 1848. *Courtesy of The Clarke Historical Library, Central Michigan University.* **Page 58:** Children's book frontispiece (Santa Claus and his "little work-people"); *The Little Messenger Birds*; Mrs. Caroline H. Butler, author; wood engraving; Phillips, Sampson, and Company, Boston; 1850. **Page 58:** Children's book illustration (Santa sewing dolls); *Santa Claus and His Works*; 10⅝"h x 9⅛"w; Thomas Nast, artist; McLoughlin Bros., New York; 1868. **Page 59:** Children's book cover, *Visit of St. Nicholas*; 10½"h x 9"w; Thomas Nast, artist; McLoughlin Bros., New York; c1870. **Page 59:** Children's book illustration (bald Santa bowing); *A Merry Christmas*; 11¼"h x 8 ¾"w; Aunt Lutie, author; multi-color wood engraving; J. C. Beard, artist; Shugg Publishing, New York; 1872. **Page 60:** Children's book cover, *Santa Claus or the Night Before Christmas*; 10⅝"h x 9"w; Wemple & Kronheim, New York; 1879. **Page 61:** Children's book cover, *The Night Before Christmas*; 10⅝"h x 9¼"w; multi-color wood engraving; J. B. Geyser, artist; unidentified publisher; c1880. **Page 62:** Shaped gift booklet (Santa exiting chimney), *Santa Claus Souvenir*; 9 ⅜"h x 4 ¾"w; Julia C. R. Dorr, editor; embossed, die cut; Tuttle & Co.; 1882. **Page 63:** Shaped advertising folder (Santa holding balloon); "William H. Frear, the Trojan Santa Claus"; 9"h x 10¼"w flat; blank back; embossed, die cut; Wells, Sackett & Rankin, New York; c1883. **Page 63:** Shaped advertising give-away (Santa entering chimney); "Compliments of Geo. Heather Fancy Goods &

etc."; 13"h x 7"w; embossed, die cut; c1890. **Page 64:** Box lid, *Santa Claus Game*; 14¾"h x 8¾"w; Parker Brothers, Salem, Mass.; c1900.

A PANTHEON OF GIFTBRINGERS

Page 67: Scrap decoration; 7"h; embossed, die cut, easel back; Germany; c1900. **Page 68:** Scrap; embossed, die cut; 1870s. **Page 69:** Scrap; embossed, die cut; 1870s. **Page 73**: Scrap; embossed, die cut; c1885. **Page 74:** Greeting card; 8¾"h x 6½"w; inscribed "1884" on back. **Page 75:** Postcard; embossed, gilded; Germany; postmarked Herrick, Ill., 1908. **Page 76:** Postcard (Christ Child in sleigh pulled by white reindeer); embossed; Germany; postmarked Petaluma, Cal., 1913. **Page 76:** Postcard (Weihnachtsmann walking alongside sleigh with Christ Child); Germany; postmarked Baltimore, Md., 1911. **Page 77:** Cigar label (Christ Child at reins of sleigh); Germany; c1900. **Page 77:** Postcard (Santa pulling sled with Christ Child); embossed; Germany; c1910. **Page 78:** Postcard; embossed; Paul Finkenrath, Germany; postmarked Dresden, 1908. **Page 79:** Greeting card; 7"h x 5⅞"w; mica frosted, silver border; inscribed "1883" on back. **Page 80:** Scrap; 13"h x 9¼"w; embossed, die cut; Germany; c1885. **Page 81:** Scrap; 7"h x 7¾"w; embossed, die cut; Germany; c1895. **Page 82:** Postcard; Germany; postmarked 1907. **Page 83:** Postcard; Germany; c1900. **Page 84:** Picture card (angel placing gifts with sleeping child); 12"h x 7⅝"w; embossed, die cut; Germany; c1885. **Page 84:** Postcard (angel helping Weihnachtsmann); embossed; Germany; postmarked Franklin, Mass., 1908. **Page 85:** Cigar box label; "Santa Noche"; Gebruder Klingenberg, Detmold, Germany; c1900. **Page 86:** Postcard; embossed; Paul Finkenrath, Germany; c1910. **Page 87:** Magazine illustration; *The Illustrated London News*; 9⅜"h x 13⅝"w; wood engraving; C. Green, artist; 1866. **Page 88:** Greeting card (Father Christmas celebrating); embossed, die-cut edge; England; 1870s. **Page 88:** Greeting card (bon vivant Father Christmas); England; 1870s. **Page 89:** Greeting card (Father Christmas riding goat); England, 1870s. **Page 90:** Greeting card; De La Rue & Co., London, England; c1880. **Page 91:** Greeting card; De La Rue & Co., London, England; c1880. **Page 92:** Scrap (green-robed Father Christmas with staff); 10"h x 5⅜"w; embossed, die cut; 1880s. **Page 92:** Scrap (red-robed Father Christmas emptying basket of gifts); 6¾"h x 4"w; embossed, die cut; c1885. **Page 93:** Greeting card (Père Noël arrives with gifts); Aubry Ed., Paris, France; 1877. **Page 93:** Greeting card (children dancing around Père Noël); Aubry Ed., Paris, France; 1877. **Page 94:** Greeting card (gnome on chimney); embossed, gilded, die-cut border; England; 1870s. **Page 94:** Postcard (Jultomten elf); G. Stoopendaal, artist; Carl Nilssons, Stockholm, Sweden; postmarked Stockholm, 1908. **Page 95:** Postcard (gnome pratfall on ice); embossed; Germany; postmarked Shelbyville, Ind., 1908. **Page 95:** Scrap (gnome with snow angel); embossed, die cut; c1885. **Page 96:** Scrap; 6¾"h x 3⅞"w; embossed, die cut; 1880s. **Page 97:** Advertising give-away hanging decoration (child angel with tree, child "Santa" blowing horn); "Magic Yeast Cakes" imprinted on back, E. W. Gilbert, Chicago, Ill.; 10"h x 8"w; die cut, metal eyelet; Stahl & Jaeger, New York; c1885. **Page 97:** Scrap (snow child); No. 998; 6½"h x 3¼"w; embossed, die cut; Raphael Tuck & Sons, London, England; 1880s. **Page 98:** Postcard (woman giftbringer); Germany; postmarked Alençon, Orne, France, 1902. **Page 98:** Postcard (woman Santa); embossed, gilded; R. Ford Harper, artist; P. Sander; postmarked Pa., 1913.

BRINGING SWITCHES

Page 101: Scrap; 6½"h x 4¾"w; embossed, die cut; Germany; 1890s. **Page 104:** Game card, "A Birch Rod"; *The Game of Kriss Kringle's Visit*; McLoughlin Bros., New York; 1898. **Page 105:** Frontispiece illustration (Belsnickle), *The Holiday Album for Boys*; Laurie Loring, author; wood engraving; Kilburn, engraver; D. Lothrop & Co., Boston; 1875. **Page 106:** Scrap (Père Noël applying switches); die cut; "Chocolat Payraud" imprinted on back; France; 1890s. **Page 106:** Scrap (Père Noël stuffing child in sack); die-cut; France; 1890s. **Page 107:** Scrap; 10"h x 5½"w; embossed, die cut; 1880s. **Page 108:** Scrap; 13½"h x 7 ½"w; embossed, die cut; Germany; 1890s. **Page 109:** Children's book illustration; *Weihnachts-wanderungen*, "Christmas Walking Tours"; Germany; 1890s. **Page 110:** Postcard; embossed; Germany; postmarked Bernardsville, N.J., 1907.

SALESMAN SANTA

Page 113: Catalog, "Lloyd & Magnus Toys, Games," New York, 1886-7; 8⅞"h x 5⅞"h; 80 pages; Peter G. Thomson, Printer, Cincinnati, Ohio; 1886. **Page 115:** Cigar box label, "Eviva"; F. Heppenheimer & Co., New York.; 1872. **Page 116:** Trade card, R. H. Macy & Co., New York; 1874. **Page 117:** Gift booklet give-away, *Christmas Stories*; Madge Elliot, author; 7¾"h x 5¾"w; multi-color wood engravings; Baldwin The Clothier, New York; 1874. **Page 118:** Trade card, G. A. Schwarz, Philadelphia; Ketterlinus, Philadelphia; 1876. **Page 119:** Trade card, "Bee Hive Great Holiday Sale"; 1879. **Page 120:** Trade card, "Wm. H. Frear's Troy Cash Bazaar"; c1880. **Page 121:** Trade card, R. H. Macy & Co., New York; c1880. **Page 122:** Trade card, "Seattle Coal"; National Bureau of Engraving, Philadelphia; c1880. **Page 123:** Trade card, "Reynolds Brothers Fine Shoes," Utica, N.Y.; Donaldson Brothers, Five Points, N. Y.; c1885. **Page 124:** Trade card, "Moore's Mince Meat"; Ketterlinus, Philadelphia; c1885. **Page 124:** Label, "F. A. Kennedy's Holiday Biscuit," Cambridge, Mass.; 4¾"h x 6¾"w (trimmed); multi-color wood engraving; c1885. **Page 126:** Counter display, "Ayer's Cherry Pectoral"; 13"h x 7"w; die cut, easel back; Dr. J. C. Ayer & Co., Lowell, Mass.; 1880s.

GETTING AROUND

Page 129: Postcard (wandering giftbringer); embossed; Germany; c1910. **Page 130:** Postcard; embossed, gilded; c1909. **Page 132:** Postcard; embossed; Raphael Tuck & Sons, London; printed in Saxony; postmarked Saline, Mich., 1909. **Page 133:** Postcard; embossed; Germany; postmarked Philadelphia, Pa. to West Sand Lake, N.Y., 1906. **Page 134:** Postcard; embossed; Paul Finkenrath, Germany; c1910. **Page 135:** Postcard; embossed; Germany; postmarked Passaic, N.J., 1907. **Page 136:** Scrap sheet; embossed, die cut; MPI, Germany; 1890s. **Page 137:** Scrap; embossed, die cut; c1885. **Page 138:** Scrap;

10"h x 7½"w; embossed, mica frosting, die cut; c1895. **Page 139:** Scrap; 9"h x 7"w; embossed, die cut; c1885. **Page 140:** Scrap (Father Christmas riding locomotive) 4¾"h x 6¾"w; embossed, die cut; England; 1890s. **Page 140:** Magazine illustration excerpt (Santa flying bat plane); Puck; Frederick Opper, cartoonist; Keppler & Schwarzmann, New York; 1894. **Page 141:** Postcard (Santa in biplane); embossed, gilded; John Winsch; 1913. **Page 141:** Postcard (Santa dumping gifts from airplane); Germany; 1920s. **Page 142:** Cigar box label (Weihnachtsmann leaving dirigible), "Weihnachtsgaben"; gilded; Moritz Prescher, Leipzig, Germany; c1905. **Page 142:** Cigar box label (Santa riding bicycle); gilded; Gebruder Weigang, Germany; c1900. **Page 143:** Postcard; embossed; Germany; postmarked Switzerland, 1908. **Page 144:** Postcard (Weihnachtsmann being driven in auto); embossed; Germany; c1905. **Page 144:** Postcard (Santa dropping off gifts from auto); embossed; Germany; c1908.

OTHER SANTA ESCAPADES

Page 147: Children's book illustration, *Santa Claus' Visit to the Schoolroom*; 10¾"h x 9"h; Minnie Douglass, author; Peter G. Thomson, Cincinati, Ohio; 1886. **Page 150:** Newspaper comic illustration, "The Mutiny of the Toys"; Sunday Supplement, *New York World*, December 16, 1900; 21½"h x 18"w; Geo. W. Peck, editor; Hy Meyer, artist; Press Pub. Co., New York; 1900. **Page 152:** Postcard (giftbringer as mailman); gelatin coating, gold stamped; Germany; hand delivered in Lancaster, Pa.; c1912. **Page 152:** Postcard (boys tripping Santa); embossed, gilded; J. J. Marks, New York; postmarked Auburn, Me.,1911. **Page 153:** Postcard (*Svaty Mikulas* - St. Nicholas - with woman on lap); greeting in Czechoslovakian; photo mechanical color; E. S. S.; c1920. **Page 153:** Greeting card (giftbringer as chef); embossed, gilded, die cut edge; c1895. **Page 154:** Magazine illustration, "The National Santa Claus"; *Judge*, December 24, 1887; 111/4'h x 18½"w; Grant Hamilton, cartoonist, Sackett & Wilhelms Litho. Co., New York; 1887. **Page 154:** Magazine illustration, "English You Know"; *The Christmas Puck*; 11½"h x 18 ½"w; Frederick Opper, cartoonist; 1880s. **Page 155:** Magazine illustration; *The Christmas Puck*; 11¼"h x 18¼"w; Frederick Opper, cartoonist; 1890s. **Page 156:** Postcard; embossed; Germany; postmarked Thomas, Mich., 1914. **Page 157:** Postcard (forest phone call); embossed; Germany; c1905. **Page 157:** Trade card folder, "The Modern Age"; Modern Age Publishing Co., New York; multicolor wood engraving; Matthews, Northrup & Co., Buffalo, N.Y.; 1880s. **Page 158:** Children's book illustration; *Around the World with Santa-Claus*; R. André, artist; McLoughlin Bros., New York; 1881.

FANTASY AND FAIRY FOLKLORE

Page 161, 167: Postcard (winter spirit and angel); c1908. **Page 162:** Scrap; embossed, die cut; c1880. **Page 163:** Greeting card; England; inscribed on back "Dec. 25th, 1881." **Page 164:** Greeting card; England; c1880. **Page 165:** Greeting card (Father Christmas dubbing "Sir Loin"); England; 1880. **Page 165:** Greeting card (Santa rising out of plum pudding); L. Prang & Co., Boston; 1885. **Page 166:** Postcard (dancing anthropomorphic objects); Germany; postmarked Denver, Colo., 1908. **Page 166:** Greeting card (Father

Christmas landscape); England: c1880. **Page 168:** Postcard; Raphael Tuck & Sons, London, England; c1909. **Page 169:** Postcard; German American Novelty Art Series, Germany; postmarked Iowa, 1909. **Page 170:** Postcard; embossed; Paul Finkenrath, Germany; c1910. **Page 171:** Postcard; embossed; Germany; postmarked Poughkeepsie, N.Y.; c1912. **Page 172:** Fancy greeting card; embossed, gilded, die cut oval border applied to scrap picture; England; 1870s. **Page 173:** Greeting card (fairy witches); England; c1880. **Page 173:** Greeting card (dancing fairies); De La Rue & Co., London, England; inscribed "1878" on back. **Page 174:** Greeting card (owls and fairies); Raphael Tuck & Sons, London, England; c1885. **Page 174:** Greeting card (frost fairies in battle); L. Prang & Co., Boston; 1884. **Page 175:** Greeting card; England; c1885. **Page 176:** Greeting card; silvered; England; c1883.

CHRISTMAS CHARACTERS

Page 179: Postcard; greeting in French; gelatin coating, gold stamped; Germany; c1905. **Page 182:** Scrap; embossed, die cut; 1870s. **Page 184:** Greeting card; gilded; England; 1870s. **Page 185:** Greeting card; gilded; England; 1870s. **Page 186:** Shaped gift booklet, "King Winter"; 6¾"h x 2½"w; die cut; Gustav W. Seitz, Hamburg, Germany; 1870s. **Page 186:** Fancy greeting card (winter character); scrap die-cut figure mounted on paper springs, embossed, die-cut edges; England; 1870s. **Page 187:** Greeting card, "The King of the Holly"; De La Rue & Co., London, England; c1885. **Page 188:** Postcard; embossed; Germany; postmarked Chicago, Ill., 1910. Page 189: Greeting card ("zip coon"); Raphael Tuck & Sons, London, England; c1885. **Page 189:** Greeting card (black child on high wheeler); England; inscribed "Xmas 1882" on back. **Page 190:** Greeting card; embossed, die cut; England; c1890s. **Page 191:** Greeting card, "A Modern Santa Claus"; 6"h x 5"w; L. Prang & Co., Boston; 1881. **Page 192:** Picture card; c1885. **Page 193:** Greeting card; Castell Brothers, London, England; 1890s. **Page 194:** Children's book illustration; *A Letter from Old Father Christmas*; shapebook, 10"h x 6¾"w; die cut; E. Lecky, author; illustration excerpt 5¾"h x 5"w; Emily G. Harding, artist; Raphael Tuck & Sons, London, printed in Bavaria; 1890s. **Page 195:** Scrap (Joey The Clown); 11½"h x 7¾"w; embossed, die cut; mounted in English scrapbook; 1887. **Page 195:** Scrap (Pantaloon); 11½"h x 7½"w; embossed, die cut; mounted in English scrapbook; 1887. **Page 196:** Greeting card (Father Christmas reviewing pantomime characters); De La Rue & Co., London, England; 1880s. Page **196:** Greeting card (clown dousing merchant); Marcus Ward & Co., London, England; c1880.

A CREATURE CHRISTMAS

Page 199: Calendar page, December, 1892. **Page 201:** Greeting card; Goodall, London, England; inscribed "Xmas 1881" on back. **Page 202:** Greeting card; De La Rue & Co., London, England; 1870s. **Page 203:** Greeting card; 8¾"h x 4"w; England; c1885. **Page 204:** Greeting card; England; 1880s. **Page 205**: Greeting card; De La Rue & Co., London, England; 1870s. **Page 206:** Greeting card; De La Rue & Co., London, England; 1870s. **Page 207:** Greeting card;

England; 1880s. **Page 208:** Mechanical greeting card; 5 5/8"h x 4 3/8"w; E. E. Griffin, poetry; frog folds forward to sit on lily pad; embossed, die cut; W. Hagelberg, Germany; 1890s. **Page 209:** Greeting card; 7 3/4"h x 4 3/4"w; L. Prang & Co., Boston; c1885. **Page 210:** Greeting card; De La Rue & Co., London, England; 1870s. **Page 211:** Greeting card, "The Kindly Robin"; Castell Brothers, London, England, printed in Bavaria; 1890s. **Page 212:** Greeting card; Eyre & Spottiswoode, London, England; c1890s. **Page 213:** Greeting card; die cut; England; 1890s. **Page 214:** Greeting card; 4 1/4"h x 6 3/8"w; England; 1880s. **Page 215:** Greeting card; 4 1/4"h x 6 3/8"w; England; 1880s.

BIBLIOGRAPHY

Beauchamp, Monte. *The Devil in Design*. Seattle: Fantagraphics Books, 2004.

Bingham, A. Walker. *The Snake-Oil Syndrome: Patent Medicine Advertising*. Hanover, Mass.: Christopher Publishing House, 1994

Bowler, Gerry. *The World Encyclopedia of Christmas*. Toronto: McClelland & Stewart, 2000.

Buday, George. *The History of the Christmas Card*. London: Spring Books, 1954.

Buster, Larry Vincent. *The Art and History of Black Memorabilia*. New York: Clarkson Potter, 2000.

Cannarella, Deborah. *Christmas Treasures*. New York: Beaux Arts Edition, 1998.

Congdon-Martin, Douglas. *Images in Black: 150 Years of Black Collectibles*. West Chester, Penn.: Schiffer Publishing, 1990.

Crump, William D. *The Christmas Encyclopedia*. Jefferson, N.C.: McFarland & Company, 2001.

Elliott, Jock. *Inventing Christmas: How Our Holiday Came to Be*. New York: Harry N. Abrams, 2001.

Fontana, David. *The Secret Language of Symbols: A Visual Key to Symbols and Their Meanings*. San Francisco: Chronicle Books, 1994.

Goings, Kenneth W. *Mammy and Uncle Mose: Black Collectibles and American Stereotyping*. Bloomington: Indiana University Press, 1994.